Essential Vegan & Vegetarian Air Fryer Cookbook UK

1200 Low Carb Air Fryer Plant Based Dairy Free Vegan & Vegetarian Recipes for Keto, Weight Loss & Type 2 Diabetes with 40 Days Meal Plan

Jenny Crawford

Copyright © 2023

Jenny Crawford

All Rights Reserved

No part of this book may be reproduced in any form without a written permission from the author. Reviewers are allowed to quote brief passages of the content of this book in their review write-ups.

Legal Disclaimer

The information in this book should not be used for diagnosing or treating any health problem. Not all diet and exercise plans suit everyone. You should always consult a trained medical professional before starting a diet, taking any form of medication, or embarking on any fitness or weight-training program.

The author and publisher disclaim any liability arising directly or indirectly from the use of this book. Always follow safety and commonsense cooking protocol while using kitchen utensils, operating ovens and stoves, and handling uncooked food. If children are assisting in the preparation of any recipe, they should always be supervised by an adult.

DEDICATION

This cookbook is dedicated to God Almighty for inspiring me to write this book.

I also dedicate this cookbook to all vegans and vegetarian air fryer users, especially beginners who wish to learn healthy, quick and easy, low carb vegan and vegetarian air fryer recipes, to help them live a disease-free lifestyle.

Table of Contents

INTRODUCTION 8

ALL ABOUT VEGAN AND VEGETARIAN DIETS FOR BEGINNERS 9

Who is a Vegetarian? 9

What are the various Types of Vegetarian Diet/Vegetarianism? 9

Who is a Vegan? 9

What are the various Types of Vegan Diet/Veganism? 10

What are the Recommended Vegan Foods? 10

What are the Foods to avoid as a Vegan? 11

What are some of the Health Benefits of Veganism and Vegetarianism? 12

What are the Nutrients to Consider on a Vegan/Vegetarian Diet? 13

Some Popular Dairy Free Foods Alternatives for Vegans and Vegetarians 13
    Milk Substitutes 14
    Yogurt Substitutes 14
    Cheese Substitutes 14
    Butter Substitutes 14
    Heavy Cream Substitutes 14
    Sour Cream Substitutes 14
    Ice Cream Substitutes 15
    Egg Substitutes 15
    Honey Substitutes 15
    Sandwich or Burger Substitutes 15

AIR FRYER TIPS FOR BEGINNERS 16

Advantages of Air Fryers 16

Air Fryer Working Principle 16
    The Rapid Air Technology 17
    Structure of an Air Fryer 17

Basic Features of an Air Fryer 17

Preset Button Cooking Buttons with Temperature and Time 18

Benefits of Using an Air Fryer 18

Common Mistakes to Avoid when Using Air Fryers 19

Air Frying Basic Steps 19

Air Fryer Buying Guide 19
    Things to Consider before You Buy an Air Fryer 19
    The Difference between Air Fryer Styles 20
    Recommended Air Fryer Brands 20

Some Healthy Recommended Oils 21

COOKING TERMINOLOGIES 22

MEASUREMENTS AND CONVERSIONS 23

Units Abbreviations and Meanings 23

Measurement Conversion Scales 23

Temperature Conversion Scales (from Fahrenheit to Celsius) 23

LOW CARB KETO DAIRY FREE VEGAN AND VEGETARIAN AIR FRYER RECIPES 24

Breakfast Recipes 24
    Squash and Cumin Chili 24
    Fried Up Avocados 24
    Hearty Green Beans 25
    Permesan Cabbage Wedges 25
    Easy Fried Tomatoes 25
    Roasted Up Brussels 26
    Air Fried Beignets 26
    Chocolate Cake with Coconut Cream 26
    Chocolate Mayo Cake 27
    Vanilla Coconut Pie 27
    Cinnamon Doughnuts 28
    Zucchini Fries 28
    Breaded Mushrooms 29
    Fried Pickles 29
    Fried Parmesan Zucchini 30
    Radish Chips 30
    Low Carb Chia Bread 30

- Garlic Cheese Bread 31
- Naan Bread with Garlic Butter 31
- Radish Hash Browns 32
- Creamed Spinach 32

Lunch Recipes 33
- Roasted Up Brussels with Pine Nuts 33
- Low Calorie Beets Dish 33
- Broccoli and Parmesan Dish......................... 33
- Broccoli Popcorn 34
- Cheesy Mushroom Slices 34
- Fried Green Beans and Rosemary 35
- Zucchini Parmesan Bites 35
- Baked Cauliflower with Cheese 35
- Breaded Jalapeno Peppers 36
- Cheesy Eggplant Lasagna 36
- Zucchini Cheese Tart 37
- Cauliflower Steak with Gremolata 38
- Broccoli Cheese Fritters 38
- Spinach Cheese Casserole 39
- Roasted Spaghetti Squash 39
- Cheesy Zucchini 40
- Zucchini and Mushroom Kebab 40
- Eggplant with Tomato and Cheese 41
- Roasted Eggplant and Zucchini Bites 41
- Cheesy Zucchini and Spinach 41
- Cheese Stuffed Zucchini 42
- Cheese Stuffed Pepper................................ 42
- Asian Broccoli 43
- Ranch Cauliflower Patties 43

Dinner Recipes 44
- Air Fried Cheesy Mushroom.......................... 44
- Cheesy Celery Croquettes with Chive Mayo ... 44
- Cauliflower Cheese Fritters 45
- Broccoli with Garlic Sauce 45
- Air Fried Asparagus and Broccoli 46
- Hot Loaded Cauliflower Steak 46
- Super Cheesy Zucchini Boats 46
- Mini Portobello Mushroom Pizzas 47
- Roasted Vegetable Bowl 47
- Greek Style Stuffed Eggplant 48
- Roasted Broccoli and Almond Salad 48
- Lemon Whole Roasted Cauliflower 49
- Cheddar Cauliflower Pizza Crust 49
- Hearty Garlic White Zucchini Rolls 49
- Vegetarian Parmesan Artichokes 50
- Zucchini Cauliflower Cheese Fritters 51
- Spaghetti Squash with Alfredo Sauce 51
- Caprese Eggplant Stacks with Basil 51
- Crustless Cheddar Spinach Pie 52
- Broccoli Cheese Crust Pizza........................ 52
- Mini Sweet Pepper Nachos 53

- Cauliflower Rice-Stuffed Bell Peppers 53
- Mushroom and Zucchini Burgers 53
- Basil Pesto Spinach Flatbread 54
- Green Cabbage Steaks 54
- Brussels Sprouts with Toasted Pecan 55

LOW CARB PLANT BASED VEGAN AND VEGETARIAN AIR FRYER RECIPES FOR WEIGHT WATCHERS 56

Appetizer, Breakfast and Snack Recipes..................... 56
- Broccoli Quiche 56
- Breakfast Sandwich 56
- Banana Bread 57
- Pepperoni Crisps 57
- Ranch Chickpeas 57
- Tofu Rancheros 58
- Battered Fried Tofu 58
- Crunch Wrap 59
- Reuben Rolls 59
- Crostini with Hummus 60
- Popcorn Tofu Nuggets 60
- Onion Rings 61
- Potato Nuggets 61

Main Meal Recipes 62
- Air Fried Fajitas 62
- Black Bean Burger 62
- Potato Cakes 62
- Parmesan Aubergine 63
- Veggie Bites 63
- Air Fried Falafel 64
- Saucy Carrots 65
- Potato Tater Tots 65
- Cauliflower Gnocchi 65
- Peppered Asparagus 66
- Lime Glazed Tofu 66
- Quinoa Patties 67
- Courgette Cakes 67
- Cornmeal Hush Puppies 68
- Potato Pancakes 68
- Tofu Sandwich 69
- Tomato Bruschetta 69
- Crispy Avocado Tacos 70
- Aubergine Fries 70
- Apple Turnovers... 71

Dessert and Side Recipes 72
- Air Fried Olives 72
- Sweet Potatoes with Maple Butter................ 72
- Curly Fries 72
- Kale Sprouts Salad 73
- Broccoli Salad 73

- Tempeh Caprese Salad 74
- Artichoke Hearts with Garlic Aioli 74
- Mushroom Skewers 75
- Sumac Roasted Cauliflower 75
- Air Fried Tomatoes 75
- Mushroom Capsicum Kabobs 76
- Buffalo Cauliflower Steaks 76
- Roasted Buffalo Cauliflower 77

LOW CARB VEGAN AND VEGETARIAN RECIPES FOR TYPE 2 DIABETES 78

Appetizer and Snack Recipes 78
- Blistered Shishito Peppers 78
- Green Olive and Mushroom Tapenade 78
- Roasted Red Pepper Dip 79
- Carrot Chips 79
- Okra Chips 80
- Crispy Spiced Chickpeas 80
- Halloumi Fries 80
- Cinnamon Apple Crisps 81
- Crispy Tofu Bites 81
- Zucchini Chips 82
- Za'atar Garbanzo Beans 82
- Potato Appetizer with Garlic-Mayo Sauce 83

Breakfast Recipes 84
- Shoestring Butternut Squash Fries 84
- Charred Radicchio Salad 84
- Roasted Peppers with Balsamic Vinegar and Basil 85
- Sweet Potato Curly Fries 85
- Roasted Yellow Squash and Onions 86
- Blistered Tomatoes 86
- Fried Cauliflower with Parmigiano-Reggiano Lemon Dressing 87
- Roman Artichokes 87
- Eggplant Salad 88
- Parsley Tomatoes 88
- Eggplants with Garlic and Parsley 88
- Perfect Broccoli 89
- Roasted Cauliflower with Garlic and Capers 89
- Tandoori Cauliflower 90
- Tomato Candy 90
- Roasted Garlic and Thyme Tomatoes 90
- Simple Cauliflower 91
- Vegetable Couscous 91
- Vegan Breakfast Ranchero 92

Lunch Recipes 93
- Air Fried Cheesy Onions 93
- Sauteed Mushrooms 93
- Tricolor Spinach 93
- Easy Cheesy Broccoli 94
- Stuffed Mushrooms 94
- Mediterranean Halloumi and Garlic Omelet 95
- Roma Tomato Bites with Halloumi Cheese 95
- Indian-Style Garnet Sweet Potatoes 96
- Easy Sautéed Green Beans 96
- Easy Cheesy Cauliflower and Broccoli 96
- Greek-Style Mushrooms 97
- Lentil Fritters 97
- Veggie Fried Rice 98
- Mexican-Style Roasted Corn 98
- Roasted Vegetable Frittata 99
- Sweet Potato-Cinnamon Toast 99
- Crisp Banana Chips 100
- Crumbed Tempeh 100
- Buffalo Tofu 100

Dinner Recipes 102
- Pepper Jack Cauliflower Bites 102
- Mint-Butter Stuffed Mushrooms 102
- Gorgonzola Stuffed Mushrooms with Horseradish Mayo 102
- Orange Tofu 103
- Golden Turmeric Cauliflower Steaks 103
- Portobello Mushrooms with Hummus Sauce 104
- Crispy Brussels Sprouts 105
- Mediterranean-Style Frittata with Manchego 105
- Toasted Coconut French Toast 106
- Pecan French Toast 106
- Oatmeal with Raspberries 106
- Corn Muffins 107
- Avocado Fries 107
- Corn Tortilla Chips 107
- Crispy Vegetable Fries 108
- Buffalo Cauliflower 108
- Cauliflower Chickpea Tacos 109
- Rainbow Veggies 109

BONUS: VEGAN AND VEGETARIAN AIR FRYER DESSERT RECIPES FOR SPECIAL SEASONS 111
- Apple Hand Pies 111
- Biscuit Doughnuts 111
- Cranberry Scones 112
- Apple Nutmeg Flautas 112
- Cheesecake Chimichangas 113
- Baked Cinnamon Apples 113
- Air Fried Brownies 114
- Air Fried Churros 114
- Funnel Cakes 115
- Chocolate Chip Cookies 115

MEAL PREP PLAN GUIDE FOR VEGANS AND VEGETARIANS 116

What is Meal Prepping? 116

Benefits of Meal Prepping 116

Common Mistakes to Avoid When Meal Prepping 117

Things to Put in Place before Getting Started with Meal Prepping 118

Some Meal Prep Success Tips 119

Getting Started with Vegan and Vegetarian Meal Plans. 119
    Tips for the Kitchen 120

Type 1 Diabetes Meal Plan Guide 120

Type 2 Diabetes Meal Plan Guide 121
    What a Type 2 Diabetic Meal Plan is Not 122

Gestational Diabetes Meal Plan Guide 122

14 Days Meal Plan for Keto Dairy Free Vegan/Vegetarian Diet Lifestyle 123
    Day 1 123
    Day 2 124
    Day 3 124
    Day 4 124
    Day 5 124
    Day 6 124
    Day 7 124
    Day 8 124
    Day 9 124
    Day 10 124
    Day 11 124
    Day 12 124
    Day 13 124
    Day 14 125

7 Days Meal Plan for Vegan/Vegetarian Weight Watchers 125
    Day 1 125
    Day 2 125
    Day 3 125
    Day 4 125
    Day 5 125
    Day 6 125
    Day 7 125

14 Days Meal Plan for Vegan/Vegetarian Diabetics 125
    Day 1 125
    Day 2 125
    Day 3 126
    Day 4 126
    Day 5 126
    Day 6 126
    Day 7 126
    Day 8 126
    Day 9 126
    Day 10 126
    Day 11 126
    Day 12 126
    Day 13 126
    Day 14 126

Meal Planner for Diabetics 128

CONCLUSION 129

INTRODUCTION

Veganism and Vegetarianism are more than just feeding styles; they are lifestyles. Vegans and Vegetarians have very high immune systems, which are very resistant to ill health or disease conditions like: cancer, obesity, high blood pressure, heart diseases, inflammation, kidney diseases, migraines, bad breath, body odour, etc. Also, low carb vegan and vegetarian diets support weight loss.

In summary, ***the healthiest vegan and vegetarian meals are the low carb meals cooked with air fryers***. This is because air fryers are one of the healthiest cooking gadgets in the market, as they help reduce the amount of oil you consume, while giving you healthy and tasty air fried meals.

I was born into a happy vegan and vegetarian family; my dad is a vegan, while my mom is a core vegetarian. I myself, am a vegan, so I shared in this ***Essential Vegan & Vegetarian Air Fryer Cookbook UK***, 1200 vegan and vegetarian meal recipes that help us stay healthy all year round.

Here is the summary of this low carb air fryer vegan and vegetarian cookbook:

- **Section 1 - All about Vegan and Vegetarian Diets for Beginners:** Types of Veganism and Vegetarianism and their Health Benefits; Recommended Vegan and Vegetarian Foods; Popular Dairy Free Foods Alternatives for Vegans/Vegetarians, etc.
- **Section 2 - Air Fryer User Tips for Beginners:** Air Fryer Working Principle; Benefits of Using an Air Fryer; Air Fryer Buying Guide.
- **Section 3 - Low Carb Plant Based Keto Dairy Free Vegan and Vegetarian Air Fryer Recipes:** Nondairy Breakfast, Lunch and Dinner Recipes.
- **Section 4 - Low Carb Plant Based Vegan and Vegetarian Air Fryer Recipes for Weight Watchers:** Appetizer, Breakfast and Snack Recipes; Main Meal Recipes; Dessert and Side Recipes.
- **Section 5 - Low Carb Vegan and Vegetarian Recipes for Type 2 Diabetes:** Appetizer and Snack Recipes; Lunch Recipes; Dinner Recipes.
- **Section 6 - Vegan and Vegetarian Air Fryer Dessert Recipes for Special Seasons:** Christmas, New Year, Easter, Harvest and Thanksgiving, Holiday, Black Friday, Independence Day, Carnival and Cultural Day Celebrations, Summer, etc.
- **Section 7 - 40 Days Low Carb Vegan and Vegetarian Air Fryer Meal Prep Plan Guide for Beginners:** Meal Prep Success Tips; Getting Started with Meal Plans; 14 Days Meal Plan for Keto Dairy Free Vegan/Vegetarian Diet Lifestyle; 7 Days Meal Plan for Vegan/Vegetarian Weight Watchers (Weight Loss); 14 Days Meal Plan for Vegan/Vegetarian Diabetics.
- **Measurements are both in US & UK Metric Units:** Air Fryer Temperature is both in Degree Celsius (for UK Users) and Degree Fahrenheit (for US Users).

Follow the tips and recipe guides in this vegan and vegetarian cookbook and enjoy a healthy, disease-free lifestyle!

ALL ABOUT VEGAN AND VEGETARIAN DIETS FOR BEGINNERS

Both veganism and vegetarianism are growing in popularity, and are seen as some of the healthiest diet styles. Vegans and vegetarians choose not to eat meat. However, veganism is a stricter form of vegetarianism, and also prohibits dairy, eggs, honey, and any other items that derive from animal products, such as leather and silk.

Who is a Vegetarian?

A vegetarian is someone who does not eat the products or byproducts of animal slaughter. Vegetarians typically consume a range of fruits, vegetables, nuts, seeds, grains, and pulses, as well as "meat substitutes" that derive from these food types.

Vegetarians do not consume following foods:

- Meat, such as beef, pork, and game
- Poultry, such as chicken, turkey, and duck
- Fish and shellfish
- Insects
- Rennet, gelatin, and other types of animal protein
- Stock or fats that derive from animal slaughter

However, *many vegetarians do consume byproducts that do not involve the slaughter of animals*. These include:

- Eggs
- Dairy products, such as milk, cheese, and yogurt
- Honey

In summary, vegetarianism is generally less strict than veganism.

What are the various Types of Vegetarian Diet/Vegetarianism?

There are several types/variations of the vegetarian diet. These include:

1. **Lacto-Ovo-Vegetarian:** People who follow this diet avoid all types of meat and fish but do consume dairy products and eggs.
2. **Lacto-Vegetarian:** People on this diet do not eat any meat, fish, or eggs but do consume dairy products.
3. **Ovo-Vegetarian:** Individuals following this diet do not eat any meat, fish, or dairy products but do consume eggs.
4. **Pescatarian:** Those who follow this diet avoid all meats except fish and other types of seafood. However, this does not meet the traditional definition of vegetarianism, and many people refer to the pescatarian diet as being *semi-vegetarian* or *flexitarian*.

Who is a Vegan?

A vegan is someone who adopts a stricter form of vegetarianism. Veganism is a way of living, which seeks to exclude, as far as is possible and practicable, all forms of exploitation of and cruelty to animals for food, clothing, or any other purpose.

Vegans strictly avoid consuming any foods or beverages that contain the following:

- Meat and Poultry
- Fish and shellfish
- Eggs
- Dairy products
- Honey
- Insects
- Rennet, gelatin, and other types of animal protein
- Stock or fats that derive from animals

NOTE: Strict vegans also extend these principles beyond their diet and will try, where possible, to avoid any product that directly or indirectly involves the human use of animals. These products can include:

- Leather goods
- Wool
- Silk
- Beeswax
- Soaps, candles, and other products that contain animal fats, such as tallow
- Latex products that contain casein, which comes from milk proteins
- Cosmetics or other products that manufacturers test on animals

Many vegetarians also apply some of these principles to their lifestyle, for example, by avoiding leather goods and products that involve animal testing.

What are the various Types of Vegan Diet/Veganism?

There are several types/variations of the vegan diet. They including:

- **Raw Vegan Diet:** You eat only foods that haven't been cooked beyond a certain temperature, usually 118 degrees F. Raw foodists typically rely on dehydrated and sprouted foods to bulk up their caloric intake. Nuts, seeds, and oils are also compliant.
- **"Raw till 4" Vegan Diet:** Here, you adhere to the raw vegan diet until 4 p.m.
- **HCLF (High Carb, Low Fat) Vegan Diet:** You eat carbs in the form of fruit, grains, and veggies and consume low amounts of fat, minimizing nuts, seeds, avocados, oils, and other high-fat plant foods.
- **80/10/10 Vegan (A raw HCLF vegan diet):** 80 percent of calories come from carbs (mostly fruit), 10 percent from protein, and 10 percent from fat.

What are the Recommended Vegan Foods?

Vegans tend to eat more fruits and vegetables than omnivores, which means their diets are loaded with fiber, plant protein, and minerals.right up arrow

Here's a list of foods that you can consume as a vegan:

- Seitan - chewy protein rich food which is an ideal meat substitute
- Baking Powder
- Baking Soda
- Dried Fruits - Medjool dates, apricots, plums, raisins, peaches, apples
- Applesauce
- Nut Butter – can be made at home using peanuts, almonds, cashews, etc. You can also buy vegan butter readymade.
- Tahini Sauce
- Low Sodium Soy Sauce

- Chili Sauce
- Snacks - sesame sticks, granola, cereal bar, crackers, vegan cookies like trail mix cookies
- Mustard
- Ketchup
- Vegan Mayo
- Whole Grains - quinoa, barley, wheat bran
- Assortment of Nuts - cashews, walnuts, Macadamia nuts, Brazil nuts, hazel nuts, peanuts, pecans
- Assortment of Seeds - chia, flax, hemp, sunflower, safflower, pumpkin, Sesame (white or black)
- Oils - coconut, olive, canola, flaxseed, and vegetable oil, as well as oils for salads like walnut oil.
- Sweeteners - maple syrup, agave nectar, stevia
- Vinegars - rice, white, apple cider, balsamic
- Blackstrap Molasses (extremely rich in calcium and iron)
- Citrus Fruits - lemons, limes, oranges, tangerines, grapefruit
- Sea Salt and Rock Salt
- Dried and Canned Beans - all varieties like pinto, lima beans, cannellini, refried beans, lentils, chickpeas, red beans, and etc.
- Tomatoes - fresh, canned, paste, diced, sauce, whole, or sundried
- Pumpkin - fresh or canned
- Canned Artichokes
- Coconut Milk
- Garlics - all varieties
- Onions - all varieties
- Potatoes - all varieties
- Rice - brown or white
- Pasta - whole wheat
- Oats - steel cut or rolled
- Nutritional Yeast
- Pepper
- Low Sodium Seasonings (Mrs. Dash brand name is recommended)
- Vegetable Broth
- Mushrooms - fresh, dried, or canned
- Vanilla Extracts
- Dried Herbs and Spices - ginger powder or root, garlic powder, onion powder, turmeric, curry power, thyme, rosemary, lemongrass, basil, dill, oregano, rosemary, Coriander, cumin, cinnamon, bay leaf, sage, cardamom, red pepper flakes
- Flours - refined wheat flour, whole wheat flour, rye, arrowroot powder, rice flour, chickpea or garbanzo flour (available in most Asian grocery stores), corn meal, corn starch, corn flour, potato starch, potato flour, buckwheat, amaranth flour, sorghum flour
- Fresh Fruits - apples, pears, bananas, cantaloupes, melons, berries, peaches, plums, watermelon, avocado, etc.
- Fresh Veggies - bok choy, cabbage, cauliflower, broccoli, Brussels Sprouts, egg plants, artichokes, asparagus, fennel, spinach, Swiss chard, kale, arugula, carrots, celery, string beans, root vegetables, lettuce, pumpkin, sweet potatoes, peas.
- Breads and Tortillas
- Tofu and Tempeh
- Vegan Cheese
- Miso
- Non Dairy Milk - rice milk, soy milk, almond milk
- Freezer Items - frozen fruits like bananas, berries, frozen veggies, non-dairy ice cream, etc.

In summary, to follow the healthiest vegan diet possible, keep in mind that eating whole, minimally processed foods is the goal. That said, there are also several mock-meat options and dairy-free cheeses available. Just check the nutrition labels of these products, as they're sometimes packed with sodium and preservatives. Some of these products are as unhealthy as animal products.

What are the Foods to avoid as a Vegan?

As a vegan, you'll want to avoid anything that comes from an animal, which includes:

- All meat and poultry products
- Seafood
- Yogurt
- Milk
- Cheese
- Cream
- Butter
- Fish
- Eggs
- Honey
- Sweets made with eggs and dairy products
- Foods that include lard and fish oil

NOTE: There are also some surprising foods that don't qualify as vegan, such as bread made with eggs, and marshmallows and gummy bears made with gelatin.

There is one caveat to the no-eggs rule: Some vegans may eat eggs if they come from their own chickens. PETA says it's A-OK if the birds producing the eggs are cared for as companions.

What are some of the Health Benefits of Veganism and Vegetarianism?

Here are some of the health benefits of adopting veganism/vegetarianism:

1. Those who adopt plant-based diets (such as vegans and vegetarians) have less of a chance of becoming obese or getting heart disease, high cholesterol, and high blood pressure.
2. Vegans/Vegetarians are also less likely to get diabetes and some kinds of cancer, especially cancers of the GI tract and the breast, ovaries, and uterus in women.
3. Going vegan/vegetarian might even help you live healthier, longer, especially if you also cut down on your daily calories.
4. Research has also proven that veganism and vegetarianism help in weight control/weight loss, as vegans/vegetarians have a lower body mass index (BMI) than people who eat animal-based products.
5. Vegan diet can improve cardiovascular health as it is significantly lower in saturated fats.
6. The diet is great for bone health, as it is high in Magnesium, which aids in better absorption of calcium.
7. Vegan dieters look younger and prevent premature aging, thanks to the high antioxidant content of the diet.
8. The alkaline content of fruits and vegetables reduces inflammation caused by acidic diets. This prevents pain in the joints and other areas of the body.
9. The detoxifying effects of the diet can be seen in the form of improved health of the kidney.
10. The high levels of vitamins C in the diet boost immunity to prevent chronic conditions and seasonal disorders. It is also of great benefit to the gums.
11. The diet does not contain cholesterol that is normally available in meat-based and dairy-rich diets.
12. Veganism is known to cause some relief from chronic conditions like migraines.
13. Vegan diet is known to benefit the overall health of the skin, nails and hair, since the diet is rich in fruits and vegetables containing antioxidants.
14. Bad breath and body odor can be eliminated by avoiding animal protein intake.

What are the Nutrients to Consider on a Vegan/Vegetarian Diet?

A vegan diet removes some sources of nutrients from the diet, so people need to plan their meals carefully to avoid nutritional deficiencies. You may need to talk to your doctor or dietitian ahead of adopting a vegan diet, especially if you have existing health conditions.

Key nutrients that may be low in a vegan/vegetarian diet include:

- **Vitamin B-12:** Vitamin B-12 is mainly present in animal products. It protects the nerves and red blood cells. Plant-based sources of this vitamin include fortified cereals and plant milks, nutritional yeast, and yeast spreads.
- **Iron:** Iron is important for blood health. Beans and dark leafy greens are good sources.
- **Calcium:** Calcium is crucial for bone health. Eating tofu, tahini, and leafy greens will help keep calcium levels up.
- **Vitamin D:** Vitamin D protects against cancer and some chronic health conditions, and it helps strengthen the bones and teeth. Regularly eating vitamin D-fortified foods and spending time in the sun can boost vitamin D levels.
- **Omega-3 Fatty Acids:** Important for heart, eye, and brain function, there are three types of omega-3 fatty acid: EPA, DHA, and ALA. Walnuts and flaxseeds are good sources of ALA, but seaweeds and algae are the only plant sources of EPA and DHA.
- **Zinc:** Zinc is important for the immune system and the repair of DNA damage. Beans, nutritional yeast, nuts, and oats are high in zinc.
- **Iodine:** Iodine is important for thyroid function. Plant-based sources include seaweeds and fortified foods.

NOTE: You may need to seek your doctor's advice on whether to take supplements or consume more fortified foods.

For more details, check out these guides:

- **What Is a Vegan Diet? A Comprehensive Beginner's Guide** at https://www.everydayhealth.com/diet-nutrition/diet/vegan-diet-guide-benefits-risks-weight-loss-effect-food-list/
- **What to know about Vegan Diets** at https://www.medicalnewstoday.com/articles/149636
- **What Is a Vegan Diet?** at https://www.webmd.com/diet/vegan-diet-overview

Some Popular Dairy Free Foods Alternatives for Vegans and Vegetarians

One of the first thing you need to learn as a vegan/vegetarian beginner is how to replace your favourite dairy foods/products with plant-based/vegan-friendly versions. **Below are some dairy-free vegan substitutes to some popular dairy products:**

Milk Substitutes

Some recommended milk substitutes for vegans and vegetarians include: Soy milk, Rice milk, Oat milk, Almond milk, Coconut milk, Cashew milk, Flaxseed milk, hemp milk, etc.

NOTE: The nutrient content of dairy-free milks varies substantially, although across the board they're lower in fat compared to cow's milk. All but soy milk also have less protein.

Yogurt Substitutes

Some recommended yogurt substitutes for vegans and vegetarians include: Coconut milk yogurt, Almond milk yogurt, Soy milk yogurt, Hemp seed yogurt, etc.

NOTE: Non-dairy yogurts can be made by adding live active cultures to an assortment of plant-based milks. They vary in their content of protein, fat and carbs. Since nutritional composition can vary greatly between brands, be sure to read the label if you're looking for a specific amount of carbs, fat or protein.

Cheese Substitutes

Some recommended cheese substitutes for vegans and vegetarians include: Cashew cheese, Daiya cheese, Kite Hill cheese, Almond cheese, Zucchini cheese, Tofu cheese, Nutritional yeast, etc.

NOTE: Vegan cheeses are often highly processed and offer less protein than dairy cheese. However, you can also make homemade substitutions with whole foods like tofu, nuts and nutritional yeast.

Butter Substitutes

Some recommended butter substitutes for vegans and vegetarians include: Coconut oil, Fruit purée, Extra-virgin Olive oil, Vegan Butter sticks, Dairy-free butter, Dairy-free margarine, Vegetable oil, Vegetable shortening, etc.

Heavy Cream Substitutes

Some recommended heavy cream substitutes for vegans and vegetarians include: Coconut milk, Almond milk, Cashew nut milk, Hazelnut milk, Hemp milk, Oat milk, Soy milk, etc.

Sour Cream Substitutes

Some recommended sour cream substitutes for vegans and vegetarians include: Coconut cream, Soaked cashews, Silken tofu, Soy yogurt, Store-bought vegan sour cream, etc.

Ice Cream Substitutes

Some recommended ice cream substitutes for vegans and vegetarians include: Sorbets, Homemade Cashew ice cream, Almond ice cream, Avocado ice cream, Coconut ice cream, Soy ice cream, Banana ice cream, Berries ice cream, etc.

Egg Substitutes

Some recommended egg substitutes for vegans and vegetarians include: Flaxseed Egg, Chia Egg, Applesauce, Pumpkin puree, Mashed Banana, Baking soda and apple cider vinegar, Baking powder and olive oil, Silken tofu, etc.

Honey Substitutes

Some recommended honey substitutes for vegans and vegetarians include: Agave nectar, Coconut nectar, Maple syrup, Brown rice syrup, Corn syrup, Granulated sugar, Barley malt syrup, Molasses, Vegan "honey" products, Date syrup and date paste, etc.

Sandwich or Burger Substitutes

Some recommended sandwich and burger substitutes for vegans include: Tofu, Tempeh, Chickpeas, etc.

For more details, check out these guides:

- **Nondairy Substitutes for 7 Common Dairy Products** at https://www.healthline.com/nutrition/dairy-substitutes
- **17 Dairy-Free Alternatives that are so Good, You won't miss the Real Stuff** at https://camillestyles.com/food/dairy-free-alternatives/
- **The Ultimate Guide to Dairy Alternatives** at https://veganuary.com/dairy-alternatives/
- **Top 13 Vegan Substitutes** at https://www.mob.co.uk/life/vegan-substitutes

Jenny Crawford

AIR FRYER TIPS FOR BEGINNERS

The problem with conventionally fried meals is that they contain excess fat. And eating excess unhealthy fat is neither good for your live nor for your health. So being able to eat fries without the fat side is just a genius idea. For most fryers we must add a spoon of oil but it's really nothing compared to a conventional fryer and its liters of oil.

The oil-free fryer allows you to eat healthy fries that will not hinder your weight loss target.

Advantages of Air Fryers

A Multifunction Device

The other advantage of the air fryer is undoubtedly its versatility. So we can, of course, make fries and a lot more. Enjoy fat-free cooking and eat healthily! You can cook the following with most models:

- Poultry Dishes like Chicken legs, Turkey cutlets, etc.
- Vegetables
- Various desserts
- All kinds of nuggets
- Seafood
- Various donuts
- Simmered dishes

You will be able to cook almost anything. This is because most air fryers come with user manuals and cookbooks.

A Safe Fryer

The fryer full of boiling oil is a real danger especially if you have children. With the Oil-Free fryer, there is no risk of splashing or spilling!

Simple to Use

Contrary to what one might think, it is a very simple fryer to use. You put your chips in the tank, you pour a spoon of oil, you close the fryer, you select your program, the total time required to cook, and you will enjoy with your guests or your family because the fryer deals alone with your fries.

Has Features to Make Your Life Easier

Depending on the model you buy, the Oil-Free fryer is often designed to make your life easier. The programmer is convenient, as is the timer. The air fryer will soon become your kitchen clerk!

Easy Cleaning

Cleaning a conventional fryer is a chore and the work is stressful. Forget this nightmare with the air fryer. All removable items such as basket or bowl are dishwasher safe!

A Capacity Adapted to Every Need

Do you live alone, as a couple, with children, or often entertain guests? Choose the capacity of your Oil-Free fryer for your future uses and needs. As an indication, a fryer with a capacity of 1 kilo allows you to make fries for 4 people.

Prices Fit Your Budget

Today, fryers have become affordable. So, of course, as for all devices, there are cheap as well as high-end, but if your budget is tight, there is inevitably a cheap fryer waiting for you.

Air Fryer Working Principle

The working principle of air fryer is very unique. While other kitchen appliances out there mostly rely on conduction for preparing meals, air fryers differentiate themselves by incorporating airflow into their cooking process in a technique called "convection." Using "rapid air technology," the air fryer can prepare meals quickly with a very minimal amount of oil.

The Rapid Air Technology

For those of you who are wondering what "rapid air technology" is, let me give you a brief overview. Once the air fryer has pulled in the air from outside, the appliance immediately superheats the air to a temperature of 392 degrees Fahrenheit, after which it is passed into a very specialized heating chamber where the actual cooking happens. This whole process is referred to as "rapid air technology" as it eliminates the need to use a heavy amount of oil during frying, baking, grilling or even roasting and completes the cooking over a very short period of time.

Structure of an Air Fryer

Different brands of air fryers out there will definitely have some "flair" of their own! However, the following features are common staples of every air fryer. In general, an air fryer consists of:

1. **The Cooking Chamber:** This is the actual chamber where the cooking takes place. The difference between various models usually comes in the form of holding capacity. Some air fryers have the capacity to hold two cooking baskets, while some can hold only one.
2. **Heating Element:** The heating element of an air fryer is the coil inside the fryer that produces the heat once electricity passes through it. Once the heating element reaches the desired temperature, air is passed through this coil, where it gets heated up and is passed towards the fan and grill.
3. **Fan and Grill:** The fan and grill of the air fryer work together in order to ensure that the heated air is distributed evenly throughout the cooking basket. The air fryer is able to adjust the direction of the air, which plays a significant role in cooking the meal consistently.
4. **Exhaust System:** The exhaust system of an air fryer is responsible for maintaining a stable internal pressure and preventing the buildup of any harmful air. Some air fryer models tend to have a filter installed with the exhaust that cleans the exhausted air, making it free from any harmful particles or unpleasant odors.
5. **Transferable Food Tray:** The food tray is also known as the cooking basket. This is where you place the food in the air fryer to be cooked. Some newer models of air fryers tend to include a cooking basket with multiple walls built inside. This makes the cooking baskets much more versatile and allows the users to cook multiple items in one go. Some models even include a universal handle that allows the cooking basket to be handled with ease.

Basic Features of an Air Fryer

Again, different brands of air fryers tend to add something special regarding their functionality in order to make their device stand out. However, the following features are common to almost all air fryers.

- **Automated Temperature Control System:** This is one of the more crucial and essential elements of an air fryer. The automated temperature control system plays a great role in determining how the final product turns out. The automatic temperature control system allows the appliance to keep track of the temperature and turn off the system when the airflow reaches a specific temperature. This allows each and every meal to be created according to the user's personal preferences.

- **Digital Screen and Touch Panel:** In our modern "digitized" generation, touch screen and digital controls are generating all the buzz! If you don't have a device with a touch screen panel, then you might as well be living in the past! Air fryer manufacturers are fully aware of this trend and have recently added a fully functional touchscreen interface into many fryers! This allows the users to seamlessly control the device without any hassle.
- **A Convenient Buzzer:** Most air fryers come with a buzzer that makes it extremely simple for users to know whenever their meals are ready. When cooking with an air fryer, you won't have to stand in front of the device all day just to make sure that your meals aren't burnt! All you have to do is set the timer and your air fryer will let you know once the cooking is done!
- **An Assorted Selection of Cooking Presets:** Air fryer companies fully understand that the majority of their users are not amazing chefs or prodigies when it comes to cooking. Some people out there are still amateur, but they want to cook and prepare amazing meals. For these people, the air fryer comes with a plethora of different preset parameters that ensure it is easy for inexperienced individuals to cook meals they can be proud of.

Preset Button Cooking Buttons with Temperature and Time

- **French fries**   400 degrees F (205 C)   20 minutes
- **Roasts**   370 degrees F (188 C)   15 minutes
- **Shrimp**   330 degrees F (165 C)   15 minutes
- **Baked Goods**   350 degrees F (175 C)   25 minutes
- **Chicken**   380 degrees F (193 C)   25 minutes
- **Steak**   380 degrees F (193 C)   25 minutes
- **Fish**   390 degrees F (200 C)   25 minutes

Benefits of Using an Air Fryer

1. Preparing meals using an air fryer will reduce the amount of oil used by 80%, but that's not the only advantage here. An air fryer is very convenient and easy to use.
2. Cleaning an air fryer does not make any mess.
3. Oil-free meals produced by the air fryer will help with weight loss and improve overall health.
4. Cooking with an air fryer will allow you to cook meals rapidly.
5. Cleaning Instructions and Some Helpful Tips
6. Some people think that cleaning an air fryer might be an exceptionally herculean task! However, cleaning an air fryer is actually very easy.

Just make sure to keep the following steps in mind after use:

1. Remove the plug from the wall and give your air fryer time to cool down.
2. Gently wipe the external parts of the air fryer using a moist cloth (dipped in a mixture of water and mild detergent).

3. Clean the outer basket of the air fryer using hot water mixed with mild detergent and a soft sponge.
7. If you see that any residual food particles are stuck to the heating element, use a dish cleaning brush to remove them.

Some Additional Tips to Note When Cleaning the Appliance:

- For maximum efficiency, soak the basket with water and dish detergent for a few minutes and rinse it thoroughly under hot water.
- Keep in mind that metal utensils and cleaning brushes may leave scratches on the body of the fryer, so refrain from using brushes, sponges or harsh products on the air fryer and its parts.

Common Mistakes to Avoid when Using Air Fryers

- If you are just getting comfortable with your new air fryer, then you should really follow the following tips to increase the longevity of your device:
- Make sure to keep your device in a well-ventilated place for maximum airflow. Keeping your air fryer in a corner will restrict airflow, which will damage your device in the long run.
- When you are not using your air fryer, make sure to remove the power cables to prevent any internal damage.
- Keep in mind that the air fryer does not take long to heat up, so preheat it just before cooking.
- When using frozen foods, make sure to thaw them thoroughly before placing them in your cooking basket (unless specifically asked by a recipe).

Air Frying Basic Steps

1. Take your cooking basket and drizzle a bit of oil in it.
2. Prepare the ingredients of the meal accordingly.
3. Transfer the prepared tray to your cooking basket and follow any additional instructions.
4. Alternatively, if you are baking a cake then you might want to put the batter in a separate dish and place this inside your cooking tray.
5. Set your temperature to the specified temperature and set your timer.
6. Make sure to check if the recipe requires you to shake your basket. If so, do it accordingly.
7. Wait until the timer runs out. Enjoy!

Note that most recipes will require little to no oil! Overall, the oil intake will be lowered by almost 80%.

Air Fryer Buying Guide

Before you conclude on the air fryer brand to buy, there are some tips you need to know about choosing a perfect air fryer brand for yourself.

Things to Consider before You Buy an Air Fryer

- **Air Fryers Come in various Styles and Sizes:** In general, basket units are easy to use and great for the basics. If you want a model that can do-it-all and then some, consider an air fryer toaster oven instead.

- **Many Air Fryers are Multi-Functional:** You can find air fryer-toaster oven combo units and even pressure cookers with an air fry function. Depending on your space and how you plan to use your air fryer, a combo unit could be right for you.
- **Air Fryer Prices Vary:** Air fryers can range in price from around $50 to upwards of $300. We've found that many of the best air fryers cost around $100 and are often on sale.
- **Make the most of your Air Fryer with Accessories:** Like the pressure cooker, air fryer accessories can help make air fryers (especially basket-style ones) more versatile.

The Difference between Air Fryer Styles

Air fryers come in three main styles: basket style, dual-basket style, and air fryer toaster ovens.

- **Basket Style:** Basket style air fryers have been around the longest and have seen many upgrades in aesthetic and cooking ability. At first, many basket-style air fryers were rounded and looked like an egg or tiny spaceship. However, the round style didn't allow for a very big basket capacity, so many of these air fryers could only fit, say, one chicken breast at a time. Today, you'll find most basket-style air fryers are more angular, which allows for more cooking space. A 6-quart model with an angular shape can easily fit a pound of chicken, making it great for families and larger households.
- **Dual Basket Style:** These models were introduced to the market in 2021 and have quickly gained popularity. Dual basket air fryers give you the option of air frying two different foods at once (at different times and temperatures), which makes them great for making whole meals or cooking in extra-large batches. Keep in mind, these models take up quite a bit of space on a countertop, so you'll need to have room for it.
- **Air Fryer Toaster Ovens:** Air fryer toaster ovens have been on the market for years and have come a long way since their humble beginnings. Many of these models act as countertop ovens that can air fry, bake, roast, toast, reheat, dehydrate, broil, make frozen pizza, proof and more. These air fryers tend to have larger capacities that can fit cake pans, quarter sheet trays, brownie pans and even casserole dishes, making them super versatile and useful for holiday cooking, if you need more oven space.

Recommended Air Fryer Brands

- **Best Overall:** Instant Vortex 6-Quart Air Fryer
- **Best Value:** COSORI Pro Air Fryer Oven Combo
- **Best Air Fryer Toaster Oven:** Breville Smart Oven Air Fryer
- **Best Dual Basket Air Fryer:** Ninja Foodi 8-Quart DualZone Air Fryer
- **Best Mid-Size Air Fryer:** Ninja 4-Quart Air Fryer
- **Best Small Air Fryer:** Dash Compact Air Fryer
- **Best Multi-Tasking Air Fryer:** Sage the Smart Oven Air Fryer
- **Best Affordable Dual-Draw Air Fryer:** Salter Dual Cook Pro 8.2L Air Fryer
- **Best Air Fryer for Versatility:** Tefal ActiFry Genius 2-in-1 Air Fryer

For more details, check out these guides:

- 7 Best Air Fryers, Tested by Food Network Kitchen at **https://www.foodnetwork.com/how-to/packages/shopping/product-reviews/best-air-fryer**
- 13 Best Air Fryers, Tested and Top-Rated by Our Reviews Experts at **https://www.bbcgoodfood.com/review/best-air-fryers**

Some Healthy Recommended Oils

If you want to maximize the "health" factor of your meals, it is of paramount importance that you use the healthiest oil possible! To save you some time and effort, I have listed the five healthiest oil that you can use while cooking using your air fryer.

1. **Coconut Oil:** When it comes to high heat cooking, coconut oil is the best with over 90% of the fatty acids being saturated, which makes it very resistant to heat. This particular oil is semi-solid at room temperature and can be used for months without it turning rancid. This particular oil also has a lot of health benefits! Since this oil is rich in a fatty acid known as lauric acid, it can help to improve cholesterol levels and kill various pathogens.
2. **Extra-Virgin Olive Oil:** Olive oil is very well known for its heart health benefits. In fact, this is one of the main reasons why the Mediterranean diet uses olive oil as a key ingredient. Some recent studies have shown that olive oil can even help to improve health biomarkers such as increasing HDL cholesterol and lowering the amount of bad LDL cholesterol.
3. **Avocado Oil:** The composition of Avocado oil is very similar to olive oil and as such it holds similar health benefits. It can be used for many purposes including as an alternative to olive oil.
4. **Fish Oil:** Fish oil is extremely rich in omega-3 fatty acids such as EPA and DHA. Just a tablespoon of fish oil is enough to satisfy the body's daily needs. If you are looking for the best fish oil, then cod fish liver oil is your best option—plus, it I also rich in Vitamin D3. But here is the thing, since fish oil has a high concentration of polyunsaturated fats, it should not be used for cooking. The best way to use this oil is as a supplement.
5. **Grape seed Oil:** Grape seed oil is a very versatile cooking oil that is extracted from grape seeds that are left behind after winemaking. This is a favorite oil among chefs and foodies! This oil has a very mild flavor that can be added with other ingredients that give a very strong flavor to meals. Grape seed has a very high percentage of polyunsaturated fat and has a similar fatty acid profile to soybean oil. According to multiple sources, grape seed oil has a good number of positive effects on the heart.

Jenny Crawford

COOKING TERMINOLOGIES

These are some of the cooking terms I will be using from time to time. It is good to familiarize yourself with these terminologies now. I also included some measurements.

1. **Beat:** To use a spoon, a fork, a whisk, or an electric mixer to mix ingredients together, using a fast circular movement
2. **Blend:** To combine two or more ingredients until the mixture is smooth and uniform in texture, color, and flavor
3. **Bread:** To coat a food in bread crumbs before frying or baking
4. **Chill:** To put the food in the refrigerator for at least 2 hours
5. **Chop:** To cut into little pieces
6. **Combine:** To put items together or place them in the same bowl
7. **Dice:** To cut into small square pieces
8. **Drain:** To remove all the liquid—may be done in a colander, strainer or by pressing a plate against the food while tilting the container forward
9. **Fold**: To gently combine a light, delicate substance (such as beaten egg whites) with a heavier mixture, using a light "over-and–under" motion
10. **Grate:** To scrape against the small holes of a grater, making thin little pieces
11. **Grease**: To coat a pan with oil or margarine so food does not stick when cooking
12. **Marinate**: To soak foods in a flavorful liquid that tenderizes or adds flavor to meat, fish, chicken, veggies, or tofu
13. **Mash:** To squash food with a fork, spoon, or masher
14. **Melt:** To use heat to make a solid into a liquid
15. **Mince:** To cut into very small pieces, smaller than chopped or diced
16. **Mix:** To stir together with a spoon, fork, or electric mixer
17. **Peel:** To remove the outside of a fruit or vegetable
18. **Pit:** To remove the seed
19. **Preheat:** To turn your oven on ahead of time so it heats up to the temperature you need it to be before cooking
20. **Shred:** To scrape against the large holes on a grater, making long, thin pieces
21. **Stir:** To mix with a spoon
22. **Strain:** To remove solid bits from liquid
23. **Wash:** To clean thoroughly (Fresh fruits that do not have skins to peel and all fresh veggies need to be cleaned with a special brush before using.)
24. **Whisk:** To use a whisk to quickly stir to get lumps out
25. **Bake:** To cook in an oven
26. **Boil:** To heat on the stove until the liquid gets hot enough for bubbles to rise and break the surface
27. **Broil:** To cook by direct heat in the broiler of an electric or gas range
28. **Brown:** To cook until the color of the food changes to brown
29. **Fry:** To cook food in hot fat such as olive oil or butter ("deep fry" means to put enough fat in the pan to cover the food)
30. **Roast:** The same as bake, but this term is used with cooking meat
31. **Sauté:** To cook quickly in a little oil, butter, or margarine
32. **Scramble:** To mix up really well (to scramble eggs, stir while they cook)
33. **Simmer:** To cook in liquid over low heat just below the boiling point (bubbles form slowly and burst before reaching the surface)
34. **Steam:** To cook food using the heat from boiling water without putting the food directly in the water—usually done with a device called a steamer (a silver bowl with holes that folds to fit many different pans)
35. **Stew:** To cook food for a long time in a covered pan, with liquid.
36. **Stir-fry:** To toss and stir cut-up pieces of food in a pan with hot oil, cooking it quickly.

MEASUREMENTS AND CONVERSIONS

Units Abbreviations and Meanings

- **Dash** = a small amount. A little less than a pinch.
- **Pinch** = 1/8 teaspoon. Taking a little between your thumb and forefinger; a little more than a dash.
- **tsp.** = teaspoon
- **tbsp.** = tablespoon
- **Pkg.** = package
- **oz.** = ounce
- **Med.** = medium
- **lb.** = pound

Measurement Conversion Scales

- **Dash** = 1/16 teaspoon
- **Pinch** = ⅛ teaspoon
- **1 tablespoon** = 3 teaspoons
- **1 cup** = 16 tablespoons
- **1 cup** = 8 ounces
- **1 pound** = 16 ounces
- **1 pint** = 2 cups
- **1 quart** = 2 pints or 4 cups
- **1 gallon** = 4 quarts or 16 cups
- **1 ml** = ⅕ teaspoon
- **1 teaspoon** = 5 ml
- **1 tablespoon** = 15 ml
- **1 ounce** = 30 ml
- **1 cup** = 240 ml
- **1 ounce** = 28 grams
- **1 pound** = 454 grams
- **1 liter** = 34 ounces
- **100 grams** = 3.5 ounces
- **1 kilogram** = 2.2 pounds
- **1 kilogram** = 35 ounces
- **3 teaspoons** = 1 tablespoon
- **4 tablespoons** = ¼ cup
- **16 tablespoons** = 1 cup
- **¼ cup + ¼ cup** = ½ cup
- **½ cup + ½ cup** = 1 cup
- **1 cup** = 8 ounces
- **1 pound** = 16 ounces
- **2 cups** = 1 pint = 16 ounces
- **2 pints** = 1 quart = 32 ounces
- **2 quarts** = ½ gallon = 64 ounces

Temperature Conversion Scales (from Fahrenheit to Celsius)

- **225 °F** = 107 °C
- **250 °F** = 120 °C
- **275 °F** = 135 °C
- **300 °F** = 150 °C
- **325 °F** = 160 °C
- **350 °F** = 180 °C
- **360 °F** = 182 °C
- **375 °F** = 190 °C
- **380 °F** = 193 °C
- **385 °F** = 195 °C
- **390 °F** = 200 °C
- **395 °F** = 202 °C
- **400 °F** = 205 °C
- **425 °F** = 220 °C
- **450 °F** = 235 °C
- **475 °F** = 245 °C
- **500 °F** = 260 °C

LOW CARB KETO DAIRY FREE VEGAN AND VEGETARIAN AIR FRYER RECIPES

Breakfast Recipes

Squash and Cumin Chili

Prep Time: 10 Minutes | **Cooking Time:** 16 Minutes | **Servings:** 4 | **Calories:** 414 | **Fat:** 15 g | **Carbs:** 10 g | **Protein:** 16 g

Ingredients and Quantity

- 1 medium-size butternut squash
- 2 tsp. cumin seeds
- 1 large pinch chili flakes
- 1 tbsp. olive oil
- 1 ½ oz. pine nuts
- 1 small fresh coriander, chopped

Direction

1. Take the squash and slice it.
2. Remove seeds and cut into smaller chunks.
3. Take a bowl and add chunked squash, spice and oil. Mix well.
4. Pre-heat your Fryer to 360 degrees F (185 C) and add the squash to the cooking basket.
5. Roast for 20 minutes, making sure to shake the basket from time to time to avoid burning.
6. Take pan and place it over medium heat, add pine nuts to the pan and dry toast for 2 minutes.
7. Sprinkle nuts on top of squash and serve. Enjoy!

Fried Up Avocados

Prep Time: 10 Minutes | **Cooking Time:** 20 Minutes | **Servings:** 6 | **Calories:** 356 | **Fat:** 14 g | **Carbs:** 8 g | **Protein:** 23 g

Ingredients and Quantity

- ½ cup almond meal
- ½ tsp. salt
- 1 Hass avocado, peeled, pitted and sliced
- Aquafaba from one bean can (bean liquid)

Direction

1. Take a shallow bowl and add almond meal and salt.
2. Pour aquafaba in another bowl, dredge avocado slices in aquafaba, and then into the crumbs to get a nice coating.
3. Arrange them in a single layer in your aif fryer basket. Do not overlap.
4. Cook for 10 minutes at 390 F (200 C). Shake the basket and cook for 5 minutes more. Serve and enjoy!

Hearty Green Beans

Prep Time: 5 Minutes | **Cooking Time:** 15 Minutes | **Servings:** 6 | **Calories:** 84 | **Fat:** 5 g | **Carbs:** 7 g | **Protein:** 2 g

Ingredients and Quantity

- 1 pound green beans, washed and de-stemmed
- 1 lemon
- Pinch salt
- ¼ tsp. cooking oil

Direction

1. Add beans to the air fryer basket.
2. Squeeze a few drops of lemon.
3. Season with salt and pepper.
4. Drizzle olive oil on top.
5. Cook for 10 to 12 minutes at 400 F (205 C). Once done, serve and enjoy!

Permesan Cabbage Wedges

Prep Time: 5 Minutes | **Cooking Time:** 20 Minutes | **Servings:** 4 | **Calories:** 108 | **Fat:** 7 g | **Carbs:** 11 g | **Protein:** 2 g

Ingredients and Quantity

- ½ head cabbage
- 2 cups parmesan cheese
- 4 tbsp. melted almond butter
- Salt and pepper, to taste

Direction

1. Preheat your air fryer to 380 F (193 C).
2. Take a bowl and add the melted butter, then season it with salt and pepper.
3. Cover the cabbages with the melted butter.
4. Coat the cabbages with parmesan cheese.
5. Transfer the coated cabbage to your air fryer and bake for 20 minutes.
6. Serve with cheesy sauce. Enjoy!

Easy Fried Tomatoes

Prep Time: 10 Minutes | **Cooking Time:** 5 Minutes | **Servings:** 3 | **Calories:** 166 | **Fat:** 12 g | **Carbs:** 11 g | **Protein:** 3 g

Ingredients and Quantity

- 1 green tomatoes
- ¼ tbsp. Creole seasoning
- Salt and pepper, to taste
- ¼ cup almond flour
- ½ cup vegan buttermilk
- Bread crumbs, to taste

Direction

1. Add flour to your plate and take another plate and add buttermilk.
2. Cut tomatoes and season with salt and pepper.
3. Make a mix of creole seasoning and crumbs.
4. Take tomato slice and cover with flour, place in buttermilk and then into crumbs.
5. Repeat with all tomatoes.
6. Pre-heat your fryer to 400-degree F (205 C).
7. Cook the tomato slices for 5 minutes.

8. Serve with basil and enjoy!

Roasted Up Brussels

Prep Time: 10 Minutes | **Cooking Time:** 15 Minutes | **Servings:** 4 | **Calories:** 43 | **Fat:** 2 g | **Carbs:** 5 g | **Protein:** 2 g

Ingredients and Quantity

- 1 block Brussels sprouts
- ½ tsp. garlic
- 2 tsp. olive oil
- ½ tsp. pepper
- Salt, to taste

Direction

1. Preheat the air fryer to 390 F (200 C).
2. Removes leaves off the chokes, leaving only the head.
3. Wash and dry the sprouts well.
4. Make a mixture of olive oil, salt and pepper with garlic.
5. Cover sprouts with marinade and let them rest for 5 minutes.
6. Transfer coated sprouts to air fryer and cook for 15 minutes. Serve and enjoy!

Air Fried Beignets

Servings: 4 | **Total Time:** 20 Minutes | **Calories:** 114 | **Fat:** 9 g | **Protein:** 3.7 g | **Carbs:** 7.1 g | **Fiber:** 1.1 g

Ingredients and Quantity

- 1 ½ cups almond flour
- ¼ tsp. xanthan gum
- ¼ tsp. salt
- ½ cup coconut milk
- 3 tbsp. swerve sugar substitute
- 1 tbsp. butter
- ¼ cup flax egg
- 1 tbsp. vanilla extract
- Swerve confectioner sugar substitute
- Cooking oil

Direction

1. Mix almond flour with salt, and xanthan gum in a suitable bowl.
2. Heat milk in the microwave then mix it with Swerve and butter.
3. Once slightly cooled, whisk in vanilla and flax egg.
4. Pour the milk mixture into the flour mixture and mix well using a hand blender.
5. Cover this batter and refrigerate it for 30 minutes.
6. Grease the air fryer basket with cooking oil and drop the batter into the basket using an ice cream scoop.
7. Add more scoops with sufficient distance in between, spray these balls with cooking oil.
8. Return the basket to the air fryer and cook the beignets for 5 minutes at 330 degrees F (160 C) on Air Fry Mode.
9. Serve once cooled and garnish with swerve confectioner sugar substitute. Enjoy!

Chocolate Cake with Coconut Cream

Servings: 8 | **Total Time:** 40 Minutes | **Calories:** 236 | **Fat:** 21.3 g | **Protein:** 6.5 g | **Carbs:** 9.8 g | **Fiber:** 3.9 g

Ingredients and Quantity

- ¾ cup coconut flour
- ¾ cup swerve sugar substitute
- ½ cup cocoa powder
- 2 tsp. baking powder
- 1 ½ cups flax eggs
- 2/3 cup coconut cream
- ½ cup melted butter
- Cooking oil

For the Whipped Cream Icing:

- 1 cup heavy whipping cream
- ¼ cup swerve sugar substitute
- 1 tsp. vanilla extract
- 1/3 cup sifted cocoa powder

Direction

1. Let your air fryer preheat to 350 degrees F (180 C).
2. Grease an 8-inch pan with cooking oil.
3. Mix all cake batter ingredients in an electric mixer until smooth.
4. Pour this batter into the prepared pan then place the pan in the air fryer basket.
5. Return the basket to the air fryer and bake it for 25 minutes on the air fryer mode.
6. Meanwhile, prepare the icing by whisking coconut cream with vanilla, cocoa, and Swerve in a mixer until foamy.
7. Allow the cake to cool and top it with the prepared frosting. Garnish as desired and serve. Enjoy!

Chocolate Mayo Cake

Servings: 2 | **Total Time:** 17 Minutes | **Calories:** 239 | **Fat:** 17.1 g | **Protein:** 6.9 g | **Carbs:** 4.2 g | **Fiber:** 5.5 g

Ingredients and Quantity

- 3 tbsp. swerve sugar substitute
- 4 tbsp. almond flour
- 1 ½ tbsp. coconut flour
- 2 tbsp. dark cocoa powder
- 1 tsp. baking powder
- ¼ cup vegan mayonnaise
- ¼ cup flax egg
- 2 tbsp. water
- ½ tsp. vanilla extract
- Cooking oil

Direction

1. Combine the dry ingredients in a 4-cup mixing bowl.
2. Whisk in the remaining ingredients to create a smooth batter.
3. Divide the batter into two 4-ounce ramekins, greased with cooking oil.
4. Place the ramekins in the air fryer basket and return the basket to the air fryer.
5. Cook them for 2 minutes on air fry mode at 350 degrees F (180 C).
6. Garnish with whipped cream. Serve and enjoy!

Vanilla Coconut Pie

Servings: 4 | **Total Time:** 27 Minutes | **Calories:** 272 | **Fat:** 27 g | **Protein:** 5.3 g | **Carbs:** 7.8 g | **Fiber:** 0.4 g

Ingredients and Quantity

- ½ cup flax egg
- 1 ½ cups almond milk
- ¼ cup almond butter
- 1 ½ tsp. vanilla extract
- 1 cup shredded coconut
- ½ cup granulated monk fruit
- ½ cup coconut flour

Direction

1. Combine all the ingredients in a suitable mixing bowl using a wooden spatula to form a batter.
2. Pour this batter into a 6-inch pie pan then place this pan in the air fryer basket.
3. Return the basket to the air fryer and then cook the pie for 12 minutes at 370 degrees F (185 C) on Air Fryer Mode.
4. Allow it to cool. Serve and enjoy!

Cinnamon Doughnuts

Servings: 4 | **Total Time:** 30 Minutes | **Calories:** 223 | **Fat:** 15.3 g | **Protein:** 9.4 g | **Carbs:** 7.1 g | **Fiber:** 6 g

Ingredients and Quantity

- ½ cup sour cream
- ¼ cup heavy whipping cream
- 1 cup flax egg
- 1 tsp. vanilla extract
- ½ cup coconut flour
- ¼ tsp. nutmeg
- ¼ tsp. baking soda
- ¼ cup erythritol
- Pinch salt

For Cinnamon Coating:

- ¼ cup erythritol
- 1 tsp. cinnamon
- ¼ cup refined coconut oil

Direction

1. Let your air fryer preheat to 355 degrees F (180 C).
2. Whisk sour cream with vanilla, flax eggs, and cream in a mixer.
3. Stir in all the dry ingredients and mix well to form a smooth dough.
4. Divide the mixture into a greased mini doughnut tray.
5. Place the tray in the air fryer basket and return the basket to the fryer.
6. Cook the doughnuts for 15 minutes or until golden.
7. Mix cinnamon with erythritol in a small bowl.
8. Sprinkle this mixture over the cooked doughnuts. Serve and enjoy!

Zucchini Fries

Servings: 6 | **Total Time:** 25 Minutes | **Calories:** 100 | **Fat:** 6.3 g | **Protein:** 8.4 g | **Carbs:** 3.7 g | **Fiber:** 1 g

Ingredients and Quantity

- 2 medium zucchini, cut into French fries shapes
- ¼ cup flax egg
- ½ cup almond flour
- 1/2 cup parmesan cheese, grated
- 1 tsp. vegan-friendly seasoning
- ½ tsp. garlic powder, optional
- Pinch salt and pepper
- Oil for spraying (olive or any oil of your choice)

Direction

1. Mix almond flour with parmesan, and all the spices in a shallow bowl.
2. Dip the zucchini sticks first in the flax egg then dredge them through the flour mixture.
3. Spread the coated zucchini in the air fryer basket and return the basket to the fryer.
4. Cook for 10 minutes at 400 degrees F (205 C) on Air Fry Mode until crispy. Serve warm. Enjoy!

Breaded Mushrooms

Servings: 2 | **Total Time:** 22 Minutes | **Calories:** 140 | **Fat:** 9.2 g | **Protein:** 9.3 g | **Carbs:** 6.9 g | **Fiber:** 2.6 g

Ingredients and Quantity

- ½ lb. button mushrooms
- 1 cup almond flour
- ¼ cup flax egg
- 1 cup almond meal
- 3 oz. grated Parmigiano Reggiano cheese
- Salt and pepper, to taste

Direction

1. Let your air fryer preheat to 360 degrees F (185 C).
2. Toss almond meal with cheese in a shallow bowl.
3. Pour the flax egg in one bowl and spread flour in another.
4. Wash mushrooms then pat dry. Coat each mushroom with flour.
5. Dip each of them in the flax egg then finally in the bread crumbs mixture.
6. Shake off the excess and place the mushrooms in the air fryer basket.
7. Spray them with cooking oil and return the basket to the fryer.
8. Air fry these mushrooms for 7 minutes in the preheated air fryer.
9. Toss the mushrooms once cooked half way through then continue cooking. Serve warm. Enjoy!

Fried Pickles

Servings: 6 | **Total Time:** 18 Minutes | **Calories:** 138 | **Fat:** 12.2 g | **Protein:** 4 g | **Carbs:** 5.8 g | **Fiber:** 2.8 g

Ingredients and Quantity

- ¼ cup flax egg
- ¾ cup almond milk
- Pinch cayenne
- 1 cup xanthan gum, divided
- ½ cup almond meal
- 2 tbsp. fresh dill, chopped
- 2 tsp. paprika
- 2 tsp. black pepper
- 1 tsp. salt
- 36 dill pickle slices, cold
- Canola oil
- Ranch dressing, for dipping

Direction

1. Whisk together cayenne, milk, and flax egg.
2. Spread half cup xanthan gum in a shallow dish.
3. Mix the remaining ½ cup xanthan gum with almond meal, salt, pepper, dill, and paprika.
4. Dredge the pickle slices first through the xanthan gum then dip them in egg wash.
5. Coat them with almond meal mixture and shake off the excess.
6. Place them in the fryer basket and spray them with oil.
7. Return the basket to the fryer and air fry the pickles for 3 minutes at 370 degrees F (190 C) working in batches as to not crowd the basket. Serve warm. Enjoy!

Fried Parmesan Zucchini

Servings: 4 | **Total Time:** 31 Minutes | **Calories:** 139 | **Fat:** 8.6 g | **Protein:** 12.2 g | **Carbs:** 5.1 g | **Fiber:** 1.3 g

Ingredients and Quantity

- 2 medium zucchini, sliced
- ¼ flax egg
- ½ cup grated parmesan cheese
- ¼ cup almond flour
- ½ tsp. garlic powder
- 1 tsp. vegan-friendly seasoning
- Avocado oil spray

Direction

1. Pour the flax egg in a shallow bowl and mix cheese, flour, Italian seasoning and garlic powder in another.
2. Dip the zucchini slices in the egg then cheese mixture. Shake off the excess.
3. Place the slices in the air fryer basket and spray them with avocado oil.
4. Return the basket to the air fryer and air fry the slices for 8 minutes at 370 degrees F (190 C).
5. Flip the zucchini slices and spray them with more oil.
6. Air fry them for 8 minutes more.
7. Cook them in batches. Serve and enjoy!

Radish Chips

Servings: 6 | **Total Time:** 33 Minutes | **Calories:** 139 | **Fat:** 6.6 g | **Protein:** 0.8 g | **Carbs:** 3.6 g | **Fiber:** 2.6 g

Ingredients and Quantity

- 1 lb. bag radish slices
- Avocado oil or olive oil, enough to coat radishes
- Salt, to taste
- Pepper, to taste
- Garlic powder, to taste
- Onion powder, to taste

Direction

1. Toss the washed radish slices with oil, salt, pepper, onion powder and garlic powder.
2. Spread these slices in the air fryer basket and return the basket to the fryer.
3. Air fry them for 5 minutes at 370 degrees F (190 C), then toss them well.
4. Air fry the slices again for 5 more minutes.
5. Adjust seasoning with more spices and cooking oil.
6. Air fry these slices again for 5 minutes then toss them.
7. Cook for another 3 minutes. Serve and enjoy!

Low Carb Chia Bread

Makes: 6 Slices | **Total Time:** 45 Minutes | **Calories:** 278 | **Fat:** 24.7 g | **Protein:** 8.7 g | **Carbs:** 6.8 g | **Fiber:** 3.8 g

Ingredients and Quantity

- 1 cup flax egg
- 1 cup almond flour
- ½ cup chia seeds

- ¼ cup almond milk or water
- ¼ cup coconut oil
- 2 tsp. baking soda
- ½ tsp. salt

Direction

1. Let your air fryer preheat for 350 degrees F (180 C).
2. Grease an 8 x 4 inch loaf pan with cooking spray and set it aside.
3. Whisk all the ingredients in a mixing bowl to prepare a smooth batter.
4. Pour this mixture into the loaf pan and place it in the air fryer basket.
5. Return the basket to the fryer and then cook for 30 minutes on Air Fryer Mode.
6. Allow the bread to cool and then slice it. Serve and enjoy!

Garlic Cheese Bread

Servings: 4 | **Total Time:** 25 Minutes | **Calories:** 225 | **Fat:** 14.3 g | **Protein:** 28.2 g | **Carbs:** 2.8 g | **Fiber:** 7 g

Ingredients and Quantity

- 1 cup shredded vegan Mozzarella cheese
- ¼ cup grated vegan Parmesan cheese
- ¼ cup flax egg
- ½ tsp. garlic powder

Direction

1. Layer the air fryer basket with parchment paper.
2. Mix parmesan cheese, mozzarella cheese, garlic powder, and flax egg in a suitable bowl.
3. Spread this mixture in a greased pan and place this pan in the fryer basket.
4. Return the basket to the fryer.
5. Cook them for 10 minutes at 350 degrees F (180 C) on Air Fryer Mode.
6. Slice and serve warm. Enjoy!

Naan Bread with Garlic Butter

Servings: 8 | **Total Time:** 55 Minutes | **Calories:** 134 | **Fat:** 10.2 g | **Protein:** 1.5 g | **Carbs:** 9.8 g | **Fiber:** 6.3 g

Ingredients and Quantity

For the Naan Bread:

- ¾ cup coconut flour
- 2 tbsp. ground psyllium husk powder
- ½ tsp. onion powder
- ½ tsp. baking powder
- 1 tsp. salt
- 1/3 cup melted coconut oil
- 2 cups boiling water
- Coconut oil, for frying
- Sea salt, to taste

For the Garlic Butter:

- 4 oz. almond butter
- 2 garlic cloves, minced
- Salt, to taste

Direction

1. Combine all the bread ingredients in a suitable mixing bowl and knead together until it forms a smooth dough.
2. Leave it for 5 minutes to rise then knead again.
3. Divide the dough into 8 pieces and spread each into flatbread.
4. Place one flatbread in the air fryer basket lined with parchment paper.

5. Return the basket to the air fryer basket and cook for 5 minutes at 300 degrees F (150 C) on Air Fryer Mode.
6. Cook the remaining bread following the same steps until golden.
7. Meanwhile, melt butter and mix it with garlic and salt.
8. Drizzle this sauce over the cooked bread. Serve and enjoy!

Radish Hash Browns

Servings: 2 | **Total Time:** 28 Minutes | **Calories:** 109 | **Fat:** 7.7 g | **Protein:** 1.9 g | **Carbs:** 9.7 g | **Fiber:** 4.1 g

Ingredients and Quantity

- 1 lb. radishes, washed and sliced
- 1 medium yellow/brown onion, sliced
- 1 tsp. garlic powder
- 1 tsp. granulated onion powder
- ¾ tsp. pink Himalayan salt
- ½ tsp. paprika
- ¼ tsp. freshly ground black pepper
- 1 tbsp. pure virgin coconut oil

Direction

1. Toss the onion and radishes with coconut oil.
2. Spread this mixture to the greased air fryer basket.
3. Return the basket to the fryer and cook it for 8 minutes at 360 degrees F (185 C) on Air Fryer Mode.
4. Transfer the cooked radish mixture to a large bowl.
5. Stir in all the remaining ingredients and mix well.
6. Return this mixture to the basket and cook again for 5 minutes at 400 degrees F (205 C). Serve warm. Enjoy!

Creamed Spinach

Servings: 4 | **Total Time:** 30 Minutes | **Calories:** 163 | **Fat:** 13.2 g | **Protein:** 7.9 g | **Carbs:** 4.7 g | **Fiber:** 1.4 g

Ingredients and Quantity

- One 10 oz. package frozen spinach, thawed
- ½ cup chopped onion
- 2 tsp. minced garlic
- 2 oz. vegan cream cheese, diced
- 1 tsp. pepper
- 1 tsp. salt
- ½ tsp. ground nutmeg
- ¼ cup shredded parmesan cheese

Direction

1. Spray a 6 inch pan with cooking oil and keep it aside.
2. Mix spinach with cream cheese, garlic, salt, onion, pepper and nutmeg in a large bowl.
3. Spread this mixture into the prepared pan.
4. Place the pan in the fryer basket and return the basket to the fryer.
5. Cook the mixture for 10 minutes at 350 degrees F (180 C) on Air Fry Mode.
6. Sprinkle cheese on top then return it to the fryer for 5 minutes. Serve and enjoy!

Lunch Recipes

Roasted Up Brussels with Pine Nuts

Prep Time: 10 Minutes | **Cooking Time:** 35 Minutes | **Servings:** 6 | **Calories:** 260 | **Fat:** 20 g | **Carbs:** 10 g | **Protein:** 7 g

Ingredients and Quantity

- 15 oz. Brussels sprouts
- 1 tbsp. olive oil
- 1 ¾ oz. raisins, drained
- Juice of 1 lemon
- 1 ¾ oz. toasted pine nuts

Direction

1. Take a pot of boiling water and add sprouts and boil them for 4 minutes.
2. Transfer the sprouts to cold water and drain them well.
3. Place them in a freezer and cool them.
4. Take your raisins and soak them in orange juice for 20 minutes.
5. Pre-heat your Air Fryer to a temperature of 392-degree F (200 C).
6. Take a pan and pour oil and stir the sprouts.
7. Take the sprouts and transfer them to your Air Fryer.
8. Roast for 15 minutes.
9. Serve the sprouts with pine nuts, orange juice and raisins. Enjoy!

Low Calorie Beets Dish

Prep Time: 10 Minutes | **Cooking Time:** 10 Minutes | **Servings:** 2 | **Calories:** 149 | **Fat:** 1 g | **Carbs:** 5 g | **Protein:** 30 g

Ingredients and Quantity

- 4 whole beets
- 1 tbsp. balsamic vinegar
- 1 tbsp. olive oil
- Salt and pepper, to taste
- 2 sprigs rosemary

Direction

1. Wash your beets and peel them. Cut beets into cubes.
2. Take a bowl and mix in rosemary, pepper, salt and vinegar.
3. Cover beets with the prepared sauce.
4. Coat the beets with olive oil.
5. Pre-heat your Fryer to 400-degree F (205 C).
6. Transfer beets to Air Fryer cooking basket and cook for 10 minutes.
7. Serve with your cheese sauce and enjoy!

Broccoli and Parmesan Dish

Prep Time: 5 Minutes | **Cooking Time:** 20 Minutes | **Servings:** 4 | **Calories:** 114 | **Fat:** 6 g | **Carbs:** 10 g | **Protein:** 7 g

Ingredients and Quantity

- 1 head fresh broccoli
- 1 tbsp. olive oil
- 1 lemon, juiced
- Salt and pepper, to taste
- 1 oz. parmesaan cheese, grated

Direction

1. Wash the broccoli thoroughly and cut them into florets.
2. Add the listed ingredients to your broccoli and mix well.
3. Peheat the air fryer to 365 F (185 C).
4. Air fry for 20 minutes. Serve and enjoy!

Broccoli Popcorn

Prep Time: 10 Minutes | **Cooking Time:** 9 Minutes | **Servings:** 4 | **Calories:** 202 | **Fat:** 17.5 g | **Carbs:** 5 g | **Protein:** 5 g

Ingredients and Quantity

- 2 cups broccoli florets
- 2 cups almond flour
- 1 cup flax egg
- ½ tsp. salt
- ½ tsp. pepper

Direction

1. Soak the broccoli florets in salty water to remove all the insects inside. Wash and rinse the broccoli, and then pat them dry.
2. Pour in the flax egg. Add almond flour to the liquid, then season witth salt aand pepper. Mix until incorporaated.
3. Preheat the airr fryer to 375 F (190 C). Dip a broccoli floret in the coconut flour mixture, then place in the air fryer. Repeat with the remaining broccoli florets.
4. Cook the broccoli floretsfor 6 minutes at 375 F (190 C). You may do it in several batches.
5. Once it is done, transfer the fried croccoli popcorn to a serving dish. Serve and enjoy immediately!

Cheesy Mushroom Slices

Prep Time: 10 Minutes | **Cooking Time:** 21 Minutes | **Servings:** 8 | **Calories:** 365 | **Fat:** 34.6 g | **Carbs:** 10 g | **Protein:** 10 g

Ingredients and Quantity

- 2 cups chopped mushrooms
- 2/4 cup flax egg
- ¾ cup almond flour
- ½ cup grated vegan cheddar cheese
- 2 tbsp. almond butter
- ½ tsp. pepper
- ¼ tsp. salt

Direction

1. Place the butter in a microwave-safe bowl, then melt the butter
2. Place the chopped mushrooms in a food processor, then add the flax eggs, almond flour and cheddar cheese.
3. Season with salt and pepper, then pour the melted butter into the food processor. Process until well mixed.
4. Transfer to a silicone loaf pan, then separate evenly.
5. Preheat the air fryer to 375 F (190 C).
6. Place the loaf pan on the air fryer basket and then put the basket in the air fryer. Cook for 15 minutes.
7. Once it is done, remove from the air fryer, then allow to cool.

8. Cut the mushroom loaf into slices. Serve and enjoy!

Fried Green Beans and Rosemary

Prep Time: 10 Minutes | **Cooking Time:** 5 Minutes | **Servings:** 2 | **Calories:** 172 | **Fat:** 7.3 g | **Carbs:** 0.7 g | **Protein:** 4 g

Ingredients and Quantity

- ¾ cup chopped green beans
- 3 tbsp. minced garlic
- 2 tbsp. rosemary
- ½ tsp. salt
- 1 tbsp. almond butter

Direction

1. Preheat the air fryer to 390 F (200 C).
2. Place the chopped green beans in the air fryer, then brush with butter.
3. Sprinkle salt, minced garlic and rosemary over the green beans. Then cook for 5 minutes at 390 F (200 C).
4. Once the green beans are done, remove from the air fryer. Then place them on a serving dish. Serve warm. Enjoy!

Zucchini Parmesan Bites

Prep Time: 10 Minutes | **Cooking Time:** 12 Minutes | **Servings:** 4 | **Calories:** 300 | **Fat:** 17 g | **Carbs:** 5 g | **Protein:** 9 g

Ingredients and Quantity

- 4 medium zucchinis
- 1 cup grated coconuts
- 1 tbsp. Italian seasoning
- 1 tbsp. almond butter
- ½ cup grated vegan Parmesan cheese
- ¼ cup flax egg

Direction

1. Allow the butter to melt in a microwave, then cool it.
2. Peel the zucchinis, then cut into halves. Discard the seeds, then grate the zucchinis. Place in a bowl.
3. Add the grated coconuts, Italian seasoning, melted butter, flax egg and parmesan cheese to the bowl. Then mix well.
4. Shape the zucchini mixture into small ball forms, then set aside.
5. Preheat the air fryer to 400 F (205 C). Place the air fryer basket in the air fryer. Then arrange the zucchini balls on it.
6. Cook the zucchini balls for 10 minutes at 400 F (205 C), then remove from heat. Serve and enjoy!

Baked Cauliflower with Cheese

Prep Time: 10 Minutes | **Cooking Time:** 26 Minutes | **Servings:** 4 | **Calories:** 239 | **Fat:** 12 g | **Carbs:** 6 g | **Protein:** 6 g

Ingredients and Quantity

- 2 tbsp. almond butter
- 4 cups cauliflower florets
- 1 cup oat milk
- 2/3 cup cooked quinoa
- ¼ cup parsley
- 4 oz. mozarella cheese, grated
- Salt, to taste
- Freshly ground black pepper

Direction

1. Preheat the air fryer to 360 F (185 C).
2. Boil water in a sauce pan. Add cauliflower florets, and then cook for 1 minute. Drain and set aside.
3. In a mixing bowl, place the cauliflower florets, and then add butter, oat milk, quinoa and parsley. Season with salt and pepper. Mix well together.
4. Transfer mixture into a casserole dish that can fit into the size of the air fryer basket. Cook in batches if need be. Sprinkle with mozzarella cheese.
5. Place the casserole dish in the air fryer basket and then fix the basket to the air fryer.
6. Cook for about 20 to 25 munites, or until cooked through and cheese is melted. Serve and enjoy!

Breaded Jalapeno Peppers

Prep Time: 10 Minutes | **Cooking Time:** 10 Minutes | **Servings:** 8 | **Calories:** 164 | **Fat:** 26.6 g | **Carbs:** 3.2 g | **Protein:** 5 g

Ingredients and Quantity

- 16 pieces medium-size jalapeno
- Olive oil

For Breading:

- 1 cup almond flour
- 2/4 cup flax egg
- 1 cup breadcrumbs

- ½ tsp. salt
- ¼ tsp. ground black pepper

Direction

1. Wash the jalapenos under running water. Then dry them with paper towels.
2. In a mixing bowl, place the almond flour, then season with salt and pepper.
3. Place the flax egg and breadcrumbs in separate bowls.
4. Coat the jalapenos by dipping them in the seasoned flour, flax egg and the breadcrumbs.
5. Preheat the air fryer to 390 F (200 C). Arrange the breaded jalapenos in the air fryer basket, such that it is not overcrowded. Then spray with oil.
6. Cook for 7 to 10 minutes or until the breadcrumbs turn golden brown.
7. Serve hot with your favourite dipping sauce. Enjoy!

Cheesy Eggplant Lasagna

Prep Time: 15 Minutes | **Cooking Time:** 36 Minutes | **Servings:** 4 | **Calories:** 350 | **Fat:** 22 g | **Protein:** 20 g | **Carbs:** 12 g | **Fiber:** 5 g

Ingredients and Quantity

- 1 small eggplant (about ¾ pounds or 340 g), sliced into rounds
- 2 tbsp. salt
- 1 tbsp. olive oil
- 1 cup Ricotta cheese
- ¼ cup flax egg
- ¼ cup grated parmesan cheese
- ½ tsp. dried oregano
- 1 ½ cups no-sugar-added marinara
- 1 tbsp. chopped fresh parsley

Direction

1. Preheat the air fryer to 350 F (180 C). Coat a 6-cup casserole dish that fits in your air fryer with olive oil, then set aside.
2. Arrange the eggplaant slices in a single layer on a baking sheet, then sprinkle with salt. Aallow to rest for 10 minutes. Use a paper towel to remove the excess moisture and salt.
3. Working in batches if necessary, brush the eggplant with the olive oil, then arrange in a single layer in the air fryer basket.
4. Cook the eggplant for 6 minutes or until soft at 350 F (180 C), pausing halfway through the cooking time to turn the eggplant.
5. Transfer the eggplant back to the baking sheet and allow to cook.
6. In a small bowl, combine ½ cup of the mozzarella with the ricotta cheese, flax egg, parmesan cheese and oregano.
7. To assemble the lasagna, spread a spoonful of marinara in the bottom of the casserole dish, followed by a layer of eggplant, a layer of the cheese mixture.
8. Repeat the layers until all the ingredients are used, ending with the remaining ½ cup of the mozarella cheese.
9. Scatter the parsley on top, then cover the baking dish with foil.
10. Increase the air fryer heat to 370 F (188 C) and air fry for 30 minutes. Uncover the dish and continue baking for another 10 minutes, until the cheese begins to brown.
11. Allow the lasagna to cool for at least 10 minutes before serving. Enjoy!

Zucchini Cheese Tart

Prep Time: 15 Minutes | **Cooking Time:** 50 Minutes | **Servings:** 6 | **Calories:** 390 | **Fat:** 30 g | **Protein:** 19 g | **Carbs:** 12 g | **Fiber:** 2 g

Ingredients and Quantity

- ½ cup grated vegan Parmesan cheese, divided
- 1 ½ cups almond flour
- 1 tbsp. coconut flour
- ½ tsp. garlic powder
- ¾ tsp. sallt, divided
- ¼ cup unsalted almond butter, melted
- 1 zucchini, thinly sliced (aboout 2 cups)
- 1 cup vegan Ricotta cheese
- ¾ cup flax egg
- 2 tbsp. full fat coconuut cream
- 2 garlic cloves, minced
- ½ tsp. dried tarragon

Direction

1. Preheat the air fryer to 330 F (166 C).
2. Coat a round 6-cup pan with olive oil and sset aside.
3. In a large bowl, whisk ¼ cup of the parmesan cheese with the almond flour, coconut flour, garlic powder and ¼ teaspoon of the salt. Stir in the melted butter until the dough resembles coarsse crumbs.
4. Press the dough firmly into the bottom and up sides of the prepared pan.
5. Air fry for about 12 to 15 minutes, until the crust begins tto brown. Allow to cool to room temperature.
6. Meanwhile, place the zzucchini in a colander and sprinkle with the remaining ½ teaspoon salt. Toss gently to distribute the salt and allow to sit for 30 minutes. Use paper towel to paat the zucchini dry.
7. In a large bowl, whisk together the ricotta cheese, flax egg, coconut cream, garlic and tarragon. Gently stir in the zucchini slices.

8. Pour the cheese mixture into the colled crust and sprinkle with the remaining ¼ cup parmesan cheese.
9. Increase the air fryer to 350 F (180 C). Place the pan in tthe air fryer basket and air fry for 45 to 50 minutes, or until set, and a tester inserted into the center of the tart comes out clean. Serve warm at room temperature. Enjoy!

Cauliflower Steak with Gremolata

Prep Time: 15 Minutes | **Cooking Time:** 25 Minutes | **Servings:** 4 | **Calories:** 390 | **Fat:** 36 g | **Protein:** 7 g | **Carbs:** 8 g | **Fiber:** 6 g

Ingredients and Quantity

- 2 tbsp. olive oil
- 1 tbsp. Italian seasoning
- 1 large head cauliflower, outer leaves removed and sliced lengthwise through the core into thick "steaks"
- Salt and freshly ground black pepper, to taste
- ¼ cup parmesan cheese

For the Gremolata:

- 1 bunch Italian parsley (about 1 cup packed)
- 2 garlic cloves
- Zest of 1 small lemon, plus 1 to 2 tsp. lemon juice
- ½ cup olive oil
- Salt and black pepper, to taste

Direction

1. Preheat the air fryer to 400 F (205 C).
2. In a small bowl, combine the olive oil and Italian seasoning. Brush both sides of each cauliflower "steak" generously with the oil. Season to taste with salt and black pepper.
3. Working in batches if necessary, arrange the cauliflower in a single layer in the air fryer basket.
4. Air fry for 15 to 20 minutes, or until the cauliflower is tender and the edges begin to brown, pausing halfway through the cooking time to flip the "steaks".
5. Sprinkle with the parmesan cheese and air fry for 5 minutes longer.
6. To make the Gremolata: In a food processor fitted with a metal blade, combine the parsley, garlic, lemon zest and juice. With the motor running, add the olive oil in a steady stream until the mixtue forms a bright green sauce. Season to taste with salt and black pepper.
7. Serve the cauliflower "steaks" with the gremolata spooned over the top. Enjoy!

Broccoli Cheese Fritters

Prep Time: 10 Minutes | **Cooking Time:** 25 Minutes | **Servings:** 4 | **Calories:** 450 | **Fat:** 36 g | **Protein:** 19 g | **Carbs:** 10 g | **Fiber:** 6 g

Ingredients and Quantity

- 1 cup broccoli florets
- 1 cup shreddedvegan Mozzarella cheese
- ¾ cup almond flour
- 2 tsp. baking powder
- ½ cup flaxseed meal, divided
- 1 tsp. garlic powder
- 2/4 cup flax egg
- Salt and freshly ground black pepper, to taste
- ½ cup ranch dressing

Direction

1. Preheat the air fryer to 400 F (205 C).
2. In a food processor fitted with a metal blade, pulse the broccoli until very finely chopped.

3. Transfer the broccoli to a large bowl and add the Mozzarella cheese, almond flour, ½ cup of the flaxseed meal, baking powder and garlic powder. Stir until thoroughly combined. Season to taste with salt and black pepper.
4. Add the flax egg and stir again to form a sticky dough. Shape the dough into 1 ¼-inch fitters.
5. Place the remaining ¼ cup flaxseed meal in a shallow bowl and roll the fritters in the meal to form an even coating.
6. Working in batches if necessary, arrange the fritters in a single layer in the air fryer basket and spray generously with olive oil.
7. Air fry for 20 to 25 minutes, until the fritters are golden brown, pausing halfway through the cooking time to shake the basket.
8. Serve with the ranch dressing for dipping. Enjoy!

Spinach Cheese Casserole

Prep Time: 15 Minutes | **Cooking Time:** 15 Minutes | **Servings:** 4 | **Calories:** 423 | **Fat:** 36.3 g | **Protein:** 6.7 g | **Carbs:** 6.8 g | **Fiber:** 5.3 g

Ingredients and Quantity

- 1 tbsp. salted almond butter
- ¼ cup diced yellow onion
- 8 oz. (227 g) full-fat cream cheese, softened
- 1/3 cup full-fat vegan mayonnaise
- 1/3 cup full-fat coconut milk
- ¼ cup chopped pickled jalapenos
- 2 cups fresh spinach, chopped
- 1 cup artichoke hearts, chopped

Direction

1. In a large bowl, mix the butter, onion, cream cheese, mayonnaise and coconut milk. Fold in the jalapeno, spinach, cauliflower and artichokes.
2. Pour the mixture into a 4-cup round baking dish. Cover with foil and place into the air fryer basket.
3. Adjust the air fryer temperature to 370 F (188 C) and set timer to 15 minutes.
4. In the last 2 minutes of cooking, remove the foil to brown the top. Serve warm. Enjoy!

Roasted Spaghetti Squash

Prep Time: 10 Minutes | **Cooking Time:** 45 Minutes | **Servings:** 6 | **Calories:** 104 | **Fat:** 7 g | **Protein:** 1 g | **Carbs:** 7 g | **Fiber:** 2 g

Ingredients and Quantity

- 1 (4 pounds or 1.8 Kg) spaghetti squash
- 2 tbsp. coconut oil
- 4 tbsp. salted almond butter, melted
- 1 tsp. garlic powder
- 2 tsp. dried parsley

Direction

1. Brush shell of spaghetti squash with coconut oil. Brush inside with butter. Sprinkle inside with garlic powder and parsley.
2. Place squash skin side down into ungreased air fryer basket, working in batches if necessary.
3. Adjust the temperature to 350 F (180 C) and set timer to 30 minutes. When the timer beeps, flip the squash and cook an additional 15 minutes until fork-tender.
4. Use a fork to remove spaghetti strands from shell and serve warm. Enjoy!

Cheesy Zucchini

Prep Time: 10 Minutes | **Cooking Time:** 8 Minutes | **Servings:** 4 | **Calories:** 337 | **Fat:** 28.4 g | **Protein:** 9.6 g | **Carbs:** 5.9 g | **Fiber:** 1.2 g

Ingredients and Quantity

- 2 tbsp. salted almond butter
- ¼ diced white onion
- ½ tsp. minced garlic
- ½ cup coconut cream
- 2 oz. (57 g) full-fat cream cheese
- 1 cup shredded sharp Cheddar cheese
- 2 medium zucchini, spiralized

Direction

1. In a large saucepan over medium heat, melt the butter. Add onion and saute until it begins to soften, for about 1 to 3 minutes. Add garlic and saute for 30 seconds. Then pour in the coconut cream and add the cream cheese.
2. Remove the pan from heat and stir in the Cheddar cheese. Add the zucchini, then put into a 4-cup round baking dish.
3. Cover the dish with foil and place into the air fryer basket.
4. Adjust the temperature to 370 F (188 C) and set the time to 8 minutes.
5. After 6 minutes, remove the foil and let the top brown for the remaining cooking time. Serve and enjoy!

Zucchini and Mushroom Kebab

Prep Time: 40 Minutes | **Cooking Time:** 8 Minutes | **Servings:** 8 | **Calories:** 107 | **Fat:** 7 g | **Protein:** 4 g | **Carbs:** 8 g | **Fiber:** 2 g

Ingredients and Quantity

- 1 medium zucchini, trimmed and cut into ½-inch slices
- ½ medium yellow onion, peeled and cut into 1-inch squares
- 1 medium red bell pepper, seeded and cut into 1-inch squares
- 16 whole Cremini mushrooms
- 1/3 cup basil pesto
- ½ tsp. salt
- ¼ tsp. ground black pepper

Direction

1. Divide zucchini slices, onion and bell pepper into eight equal portions. Place on 6-inch skewers for a total of eight kebabs.
2. Add 2 mushrooms to each skewer and brush generously with pesto.
3. Sprinkle each kebab with salt and black pepper on all sides, then place into ungreased air fryer basket.
4. Adjust the temperature to 375 F (190 C) and set timer to 8 minutes, flipping the kebabs when cooked halfway through.
5. Vegetables will be browned at the edges and tender-crisp when done. Serve warm. Enjoy!

Eggplant with Tomato and Cheese

Prep Time: 5 Minutes | **Cooking Time:** 35 Minutes | **Servings:** 4 | **Calories:** 306 | **Fat:** 16.1 g | **Protein:** 39.6 g | **Carbs:** 7 g | **Fiber:** 1.8 g

Ingredients and Quantity

- 1 eggplant, peeled and sliced
- 2 bell peppers, seeded and sliced
- 1 red onion, sliced
- 1 tsp. fresh garlic, minced
- 4 tbsp. olive oil
- 1 tsp. mustard
- 1 tsp. dried oregano
- 1 tsp. smoked paprika
- Salt and ground black pepper, to taste
- 1 tomato, sliced
- 6 oz. (170 g) vegan Halloumi cheese, sliced lengthwise

Direction

1. Preheat the air fryer to 370 F (188 C). Spritz a baking pan with non-stick cooking spray.
2. Place the eggplant, peppers, onion and garlic on the bottom of the baking pan. Add the olive oil, mustard and spices.
3. Transfer to the air fryer basket and cook for 14 minutes.
4. Top with the sliced tomatoes and cheese.
5. Increase the temperature to 390 F (199 C) and cook for 5 minutes more until bubbling starts.
6. Allow to sit on a cooking rack for 10 minutes until before serving. Enjoy!

Roasted Eggplant and Zucchini Bites

Prep Time: 35 Minutes | **Cooking Time:** 30 Minutes | **Servings:** 8 | **Calories:** 110 | **Fat:** 8.3 g | **Protein:** 2.6 g | **Carbs:** 6.3 g | **Fiber:** 2.5 g

Ingredients and Quantity

- 2 tsp. fresh mint leaves, chopped
- 1 ½ tsp. red pepper chili flakes
- 2 tbsp. melted almond butter
- 1 pound (454 g) eggplant, peeled and cubed
- 1 pound (454 g) zucchini, peeled and cubed
- 3 tbsp. olive oil

Direction

1. Toss all the above ingredients in a large-sized mixing dish.
2. Roast the eggplant and zucchini bites for 30 minutes at 325 F (163 C) in your air fryer, flipping once or twice.
3. Serve with homemade dipping sauce. Enjoy!

Cheesy Zucchini and Spinach

Prep Time: 9 Minutes | **Cooking Time:** 7 Minutes | **Servings:** 6 | **Calories:** 171 | **Fat:** 10.8 g | **Protein:** 3.1 g | **Carbs:** 14.9 g | **Fiber:** 1 g

Ingredients and Quantity

- 1 cup applesauce
- ½ cup almond flour
- ½ cup vegan Ricotta cheese, crumbled
- 1 tsp. fine sea salt
- 4 garlic cloves, minced
- 1 cup baby spinach
- ½ cup Parmesan cheese, grated
- 1/3 tsp. red pepper flakes
- 1 pound (454 g) zucchini, peeled and grated
- 1/3 tsp. dried dill weed

Direction

1. Thoroughly combine all the ingredients in a mixing bowl. Now, roll the mixture to form small Croquettes.
2. Air fry for 335 F (168 C) for 7 minutes or until golden.
3. Taste, adjust for seasoning and serve warm. Enjoy!

Cheese Stuffed Zucchini

Prep Time: 20 Minutes | **Cooking Time:** 8 Minutes | **Servings:** 4 | **Calories:** 199 | **Fat:** 16.4 g | **Protein:** 9.2 g | **Carbs:** 4 g | **Fiber:** 0.5 g

Ingredients and Quantity

- 1 large zucchini, cut into 4 pieces
- 2 tbsp. olive oil
- 1 cup vegan Ricotta cheese, at room temperature
- 2 tbsp. scallions, chopped
- 1 heaping tbsp. fresh parsley, roughly chopped
- 1 heaping tbsp. coriander, minced
- 2 oz. (57 g) vegan Cheddar cheese, preferably freshly grated
- 1 tsp. celery seeds
- ½ tsp. salt
- ½ tsp. garlic pepper

Direction

1. Cook the zucchini in the air fryer at 350 F (180 C) for approximately 10 minutes. Check for doneness and cook for extra 2 to 3 minutes if necessary.
2. Meanwhile, make the stuffing by mixing the other ingredients in a mixing bowl.
3. When your zucchini is thoroughly cooked, open them up. Divide the stuffing among all the zucchini pieces and stuff the zucchinis with the stuffing.
4. Bake them for an additional 5 minutes in your air fryer. Serve and enjoy!

Cheese Stuffed Pepper

Prep Time: 20 Minutes | **Cooking Time:** 15 Minutes | **Servings:** 2 | **Calories:** 360 | **Fat:** 27.3 g | **Protein:** 20.3 g | **Carbs:** 6.4 g | **Fiber:** 1.2 g

Ingredients and Quantity

- 1 red bell pepper, top and seeds removed
- 1 yellow bell pepper, top and seeds removed
- Salt and pepper, to taste
- 1 cup vegan Ricotta cheese
- 4 tbsp. vegan mayonnaise
- 2 pickles, chopped

Direction

1. Arrange the peppers in a slightly greased air fryer basket.
2. Cook in the preheated air fryer at 400 F (205 C) for 15 minutes, flipping them over halfway through the cooking time.
3. Season with salt and pepper.
4. Then in a mixing bowl, combine the cream cheese with the mayonnaise and chopped pickles.
5. Stuff the peppers with the cream cheese mixture and serve. Enjoy!

Asian Broccoli

Servings: 2 | **Total Time:** 36 Minutes | **Calories:** 189 | **Fat:** 10.9 g | **Protein:** 6.2 g | **Carbs:** 4.1 g | **Fiber:** 7 g

Ingredients and Quantity

- 1 lb. broccoli, cut into florets
- 1 ½ tbsp. olive oil
- 1 tbsp. garlic, minced
- Salt, to taste
- 2 tbsp. reduced sodium soy sauce
- 2 tsp. sriracha
- 1 tsp. rice vinegar
- Fresh lime juice, optional

Direction

1. Toss the broccoli with garlic, salt and oil in a large bowl.
2. Spread the coated broccoli in the air fryer basket and return and return the basket to the air fryer
3. Cook them for 20 minutes at 400 degrees F (205 C) until golden Air Fryer Mode.
4. Toss the broccoli once cooked half way through.
5. Mix sriracha, rice vinegar, and soy sauce in a small bowl.
6. Heat this mixture in the microwave for 15 seconds until mixed and melted.
7. Toss the cooked broccoli with soy sauce mixture in a large bowl.
8. Mix well and adjust seasoning with salt.
9. Add lime juice. Serve and enjoy!

Ranch Cauliflower Patties

Servings: 2 | **Total Time:** 35 Minutes | **Calories:** 201 | **Fat:** 7.8 g | **Protein:** 7.8 g | **Carbs:** 4.1 g | **Fiber:** 9.7 g

Ingredients and Quantity

- 2 cup cauliflower florets, grated
- 1 green onion, chopped
- 1 tsp. minced garlic
- 2 tbsp. organic ranch seasoning mix
- 1 cup packed cilantro
- ½ tsp. chili powder
- ¼ tsp. cumin
- 2 tbsp. xanthan gum
- ¼ cup ground flaxseed
- ¼ cup sunflower seeds
- ¼ tsp. Kosher salt and pepper
- Dipping sauce of your choice

Direction

1. Let your air fryer preheat to 400 degrees F (205 C). Grease the basket with cooking oil.
2. Toss all the vegetables in a food processor and grind them together.
3. Add flaxseed, sunflower seeds, all the seasoning, xanthan gum, and cilantro.
4. Mix well until it forms a thick batter.
5. Make 1.5-inch thick patties out of it.
6. Place 4 patties in the air fryer basket then return the basket to the air fryer.
7. Cook them for 20 minutes on Air Fry Mode, flipping them halfway through.
8. Cook the remaining patties using the same steps. Serve and enjoy!

Dinner Recipes

Air Fried Cheesy Mushroom

Prep Time: 10 Minutes | **Cooking Time:** 14 Minutes | **Servings:** 4 | **Calories:** 270 | **Fat:** 23 g | **Protein:** 8 g | **Carbs:** 7 g | **Fiber:** 4 g

Ingredients and Quantity

- 2 tbsp. olive oil
- 4 large Portobello mushrooms, stems removed and gills scraped out
- ½ tsp. salt
- ¼ tsp. freshly ground pepper
- 4 oz. (113 g) vegan Ricotta cheese, crumbled
- ½ cup frozen spinach, thawed and squeezed dry
- ½ cup chopped marinated artichoke hearts
- ½ cup grated vegan Parmesan cheese
- 2 tbsp. chopped fresh parsley

Direction

1. Preheat the air fryer to 400 F (205 C).
2. Rub the olive oil over the Portobello mushrooms until thoroughly coated. Sprinkle both sides with salt and pepper. Place top-side down on a clean work surface.
3. In a small bowl, combine the Ricotta cheese, artichoke hearts and spinach. Mash with the back of a fork until thoroughly combined.
4. Divide the cheese mixture among the mushrooms and sprinkle with Parmesan cheese.
5. Air fry for 10 to 14 minutes, until the mushrooms are tender and the cheese has begun to brown.
6. Top with the fresh parsley just before serving. Enjoy!

Cheesy Celery Croquettes with Chive Mayo

Prep Time: 15 Minutes | **Cooking Time:** 6 Minutes | **Servings:** 4 | **Calories:** 214 | **Fat:** 18 g | **Protein:** 7 g | **Carbs:** 5.2 g | **Fiber:** 1.6 g

Ingredients and Quantity

- 2 medium-sized celery stalks, trimmed and grated
- ½ cup leek, finely chopped
- 1 tbsp. garlic paste
- ¼ tsp. freshly cracked black pepper
- 1 tsp. fine sea salt
- 1 tbsp. fresh dill, finely chopped
- ¼ cup applesauce
- ¼ cup almond flour
- ½ cup vegan Parmesan cheese, freshly grated
- ¼ tsp. baking powder
- 2 tbsp. fresh chives, chopped
- 4 tbsp. vegan mayonnaise

Direction

1. Place the celery on a paper towel and squeeze them to remove excess liquid.
2. Combine the vegetables with the other ingredients, except the chives and mayo. Shape into balls usning 1 tablespoon of the vegetable mixture.
3. Then gently flatten each ball with your palm or a wide spatula. Spritz the croquettes with a non-stick cooking oil.
4. Air fry the vegetable croquettes in a single layer for 6 minutes at 360 F (182 C).

5. Meanwhile, mix the fresh chives and mayonnaise. Serve the croquettes warm with the chive mayo. Enjoy!

Cauliflower Cheese Fritters

Prep Time: 15 Minutes | **Cooking Time:** 10 Minutes | **Servings:** 8 | **Calories:** 282 | **Fat:** 22 g | **Protein:** 12 g | **Carbs:** 6 g | **Fiber:** 2 g

Ingredients and Quantity

- 2 pounds (907 g) cauliflower florets
- ½ cup scallions, finely chopped
- ½ tsp. freshly ground black pepper, or to taste
- 1 tbsp. fine sea salt
- ½ tsp. hot paprika
- 2 cups Violife cheese, shredded
- 1 cup vegan Parmesan cheese, grated
- ¼ cup olive oil

Direction

1. Firstly, boil the cauliflower until fork tender. Drain, peel and mash the cooked cauliflower.
2. Thoroughly mix the mashed cauliflower with scallions, pepper, salt, paprika and Violife cheese.
3. Then shape into balls using your hands. Now flatten the balls to make the patties.
4. Roll the patties over grated Parmesan cheese. Drizzle olive oil over them.
5. Next, cook the patties at 360 F (182 C) for approximately 10 minutes, working in batches if necessary.
6. Serve with vegan mayo if you wish. Enjoy!

Broccoli with Garlic Sauce

Prep Time: 19 Minutes | **Cooking Time:** 15 Minutes | **Servings:** 4 | **Calories:** 247 | **Fat:** 22 g | **Protein:** 4 g | **Carbs:** 6 g | **Fiber:** 3 g

Ingredients and Quantity

- 2 tbsp. olive oil
- Kosher salt and freshly ground black pepper, to taste
- 1 pound (454 g) broccoli florets

For the Dipping Sauce:

- 2 tsp. dried rosemary, crushed
- 3 garlic cloves, minced
- 1/3 tsp. dried marjoram, crushed
- ¼ cup full-fat coconut milk
- 1/3 cup vegan mayonnaise

Direction

1. Lightly grease your broccoli with a thin layer of olive oil. Season with salt and black pepper.
2. Arrange the seasoned broccoli in an air fryer basket. Bake at 395 F (202 C) for 15 minutes, shaking once or twice.
3. In the meantime, prepare the dipping sauce by mixing all the sauce ingredients.
4. Serve broccoli warm with the dipping sauce. Enjoy!

Air Fried Asparagus and Broccoli

Prep Time: 25 Minutes | **Cooking Time:** 22 Minutes | **Servings:** 4 | **Calories:** 181 | **Fat:** 7 g | **Protein:** 3 g | **Carbs:** 1 g | **Fiber:** 3 g

Ingredients and Quantity

- ½ pound (227 g) asparagus, cut into 1 ½-inch pieces
- ½ pound (227 g) broccoli, cut into 1 ½-inch pieces
- 2 tbsp. olive oil
- Salt and white pepper, to taste
- ½ cup vegetable broth
- 2 tbsp. apple cider vinegar

Direction

1. Place the vegetables in a single layer in the lightly grease air fryer basket.
2. Drizzle the olive oil over the vegetables. Sprinkle with salt and white pepper.
3. Cook at 380 F (193 C) for 15 minutes, shaking the basket halfway through the cooking time.
4. Add ½ cup of vegetable broth to a saucepan, bring to a rapid boil and add the vinegar. Cook for about 5 to 7 minutes, or until the sauce has reduced by half.
5. Spoon the sauce over the warm vegetables and serve immediately. Enjoy!

Hot Loaded Cauliflower Steak

Prep Time: 5 Minutes | **Cooking Time:** 7 Minutes | **Servings:** 4 | **Calories:** 122 | **Fat:** 8 g | **Protein:** 5 g | **Carbs:** 5 g | **Fiber:** 2 g

Ingredients and Quantity

- 1 medium-size head cauliflower
- ¼ cup vegan hot sauce
- 2 tbsp. salted almond butter, melted
- ¼ cup vegan blue cheese crumbles
- ¼ cup full-fat ranch dressing

Direction

1. Remove cauliflower leaves. Slice the head in ½-inch thick slices.
2. In a small bowl, mix hot sauce and butter. Brush the mixture over the cauliflower.
3. Place each cauliflower steak into the air fryer basket, working in batches if necessary.
4. Adjust the temperature to 400 F (205 C) and air fry for 7 minutes.
5. When cooked, the edges of the cauliflower will begin turning dark and caramelized.
6. To serve, sprinkle steaks with crumbled blue cheese. Drizzle with ranch dressing. Enjoy!

Super Cheesy Zucchini Boats

Prep Time: 15 Minutes | **Cooking Time:** 20 Minutes | **Servings:** 2 | **Calories:** 215 | **Fat:** 15 g | **Protein:** 10 g | **Carbs:** 6 g | **Fiber:** 3 g

Ingredients and Quantity

- 2 medium-size zucchini
- 1 tbsp. avocado oil

- ¼ cup low carb, no-sugar-added pasta sauce
- ¼ cup full-fat Ricotta cheese
- ¼ cup shredded Mozzarella cheese
- ¼ tsp. dried oregano
- ¼ tsp. garlic powder
- ½ tsp. dried parsley
- 2 tbsp. grated vegetarian Parmesan cheese

Direction

1. Cut off 1 inch from the top and bottom of each zucchini.
2. Slice zucchini in half lengthwise and use a spoon to scoop out a bit of the inside, making room for filling.
3. Brush with avocado oil and spoon 2 tablespoon pasta sauce into each zucchini shell.
4. In a medium bowl, mix the Ricotta, Mozzarella, oregano, garlic powder and parsley. Spoon the mixture into each zucchini shell.
5. Place the stuffed zucchini shells into the air fryer basket. Adjust the temperature to 350 F (177 C) and air fry for 20 minutes.
6. To remove from the air fryer basket, use tongs or a spatula and carefully lift out.
7. Top with Parmesan cheese. Serve immediately. Enjoy!

Mini Portobello Mushroom Pizzas

Prep Time: 10 Minutes | **Cooking Time:** 10 Minutes | **Servings:** 2 | **Calories:** 244 | **Fat:** 18 g | **Protein:** 10 g | **Carbs:** 5 g | **Fiber:** 2 g

Ingredients and Quantity

- 2 large Portobello mushrooms
- 2 tbsp. unsalted almond butter, melted
- ½ tsp. garlic powder
- 2/3 cup shredded Mozzarella cheese
- 4 grape tomatoes, sliced
- 2 fresh basil leaves, chopped
- 1 tbsp. balsamic vinegar

Direction

1. Scoop out the inside of the mushrooms, leaving just the caps. Brush each cap with butter and sprinkle with garlic powder.
2. Fill each cap with Mozzarella and sliced tomatoes.
3. Place each mini pizza into a round baking pan. Then place the pan into the air fryer.
4. Adjust temperature to 380 F (193 C) and air fry for 10 minutes.
5. Carefully remove the pizzas from the air fryer basket and garnish with basil and a drizzle of vinegar. Serve and enjoy!

Roasted Vegetable Bowl

Prep Time: 10 Minutes | **Cooking Time:** 15 Minutes | **Servings:** 2 | **Calories:** 121 | **Fat:** 7 g | **Protein:** 4 g | **Carbs:** 8 g | **Fiber:** 5 g

Ingredients and Quantity

- 1 cup broccoli florets
- 1 cup quartered Brussels sprouts
- ½ cup cauliflower florets
- ¼ medium-size white onion, peeled and sliced ¼ inch thick
- ½ medium size green bell pepper, seeded and sliced ¼ inch thick
- 1 tbsp. coconut oil

- 2 tbsp. chili powder
- ½ tsp. garlic powder
- ½ tsp. cumin

Direction

1. Toss all the ingredients together in a large bowl until vegetables are fully coated with oil and seasoning.
2. Pour the vegetables into the air fryer basket.
3. Adjust the temperature to 360 F (182 C) and roast for 15 minutes.
4. Shake two or three times during cooking. Serve warm. Enjoy!

Greek Style Stuffed Eggplant

Prep Time: 15 Minutes | **Cooking Time:** 20 Minutes | **Servings:** 2 | **Calories:** 291 | **Fat:** 19 g | **Protein:** 9 g | **Carbs:** 12 g | **Fiber:** 11 g

Ingredients and Quantity

- 1 large eggplant
- 2 tbsp. unsalted almond butter
- ¼ medium-size yellow onion, diced
- ¼ cup artichoke hearts
- 1 cup fresh spinach
- 2 tbsp. diced red bell pepper
- ½ cup crumbled vegan Ricotta cheese

Direction

1. Slice the eggplant in half lengthwise and scoop out the flesh, leaving enough inside for the shell to remain intact.
2. Take the eggplant flesh that was scooped out, chop and set aside.
3. In a medium skillet over medium heat, add butter and onion. Saute until onions begin to soften, about 3 to 5 minutes.
4. Add the chopped eggplant flesh, artichokes, spinach and bell pepper.
5. Cook until peppers soften and spinach wilts. Remove from the heat and gently fold in the Ricotta cheese.
6. Place the filling into each eggplant shell and place into the air fryer basket.
7. Adjust the temperature to 320 F (160 C) and air fry for 20 minutes.
8. Eggplant will be tender when done. Serve warm. Enjoy!

Roasted Broccoli and Almond Salad

Prep Time: 10 Minutes | **Cooking Time:** 7 Minutes | **Servings:** 2 | **Calories:** 215 | **Fat:** 16 g | **Protein:** 6 g | **Carbs:** 8 g | **Fiber:** 4 g

Ingredients and Quantity

- 3 cups fresh broccoli florets
- 2 tbsp. salted almond butter, melted
- ¼ cup sliced almonds
- ½ medium-size lemon

Direction

1. Place the broccoli into a round baking dish. Pour butter over the broccoli. Add almonds and toss.
2. Place the dish into the air fryer basket. Adjust the temperature to 380 F (193 C) and bake for 7 minutes.
3. Stir halfway through the cooking time.
4. When done, zest lemon onto broccoli and squeeze juice into pan. Serve warm. Enjoy!

Lemon Whole Roasted Cauliflower

Prep Time: 5 Minutes | **Cooking Time:** 15 Minutes | **Servings:** 4 | **Calories:** 91 | **Fat:** 6 g | **Protein:** 3 g | **Carbs:** 5 g | **Fiber:** 3 g

Ingredients and Quantity

- 1 medium-size head cauliflower
- 2 tbsp. salted almond butter, melted
- 1 medium-size lemon
- ½ tsp. garlic powder
- 1 tsp. dried parsley

Direction

1. Remove the leaves from the head of cauliflower and brush it with the melted butter.
2. Cut the lemon in half and zest one half onto the cauliflower. Squeeze the juice of the zested lemon half and pour it over the cauliflower.
3. Sprinkle with garlic powder and parsley. Place cauliflower head into the air fryer basket.
4. Adjust the temperature to 350 F (177 C) and air fry for 15 minutes.
5. Check the cauliflower every 5 minutes to avoid overcooking. When done, it should be fork tender.
6. To serve, squeeze juice from the other lemon half over the cauliflower. Serve immediately. Enjoy!

Cheddar Cauliflower Pizza Crust

Prep Time: 15 Minutes | **Cooking Time:** 11 Minutes | **Servings:** 2 | **Calories:** 230 | **Fat:** 14 g | **Protein:** 15 g | **Carbs:** 5 g | **Fiber:** 5 g

Ingredients and Quantity

- 1 (12 oz. or 340 g) steamer bag cauliflower
- ½ cup shredded vegan Cheddar cheese
- ¼ cup applesauce
- 2 tbsp. blanched finely ground almond flour
- 1 tsp. Italian blend seasoning

Direction

1. Cook the cauliflower according to package instructions.
2. Remove from bag and place into cheesecloth or paper towel to remove excess water. Place the cauliflower into a large bowl.
3. Add the cheese, applesauce, almond flour and Italian seasoning to the bowl and mix well.
4. Cut a piece of parchment to fit your air fryer basket. Press cauliflower into 6-inch round circle. Then place into the air fryer basket.
5. Adjust the temperature to 360 F (182 C) and air fry for 11 minutes, flipping the pizza crust after the first 7 minutes of cooking time.
6. Add preferred toppings to the pizza. Place back into the air fryer basket and cook for an additional 4 minutes, or until fully cooked and golden. Serve immediately. Enjoy!

Hearty Garlic White Zucchini Rolls

Prep Time: 20 Minutes | **Cooking Time:** 20 Minutes | **Servings:** 4 | **Calories:** 245 | **Fat:** 19 g | **Protein:** 10 g | **Carbs:** 5 g | **Fiber:** 2 g

Ingredients and Quantity

- 2 medium-size zucchini
- 2 tbsp. unsalted almond butter
- ¼ white onion, peeled and diced
- ½ tsp. finely minced roasted garlic
- ¼ cup coconut cream
- 2 tbsp. vegetable broth
- 1/8 tsp. xanthan gum
- ½ cup full-fat Ricotta cheese
- ¼ tsp. salt
- ½ tsp. garlic powder
- ¼ tsp. dried oregano
- 2 cups spinach, chopped
- ½ cup sliced baby Portobello mushrooms
- ¾ shredded vegan Mozzarella cheese, divided

Direction

1. Using a mandoline or a sharp knife, slice zucchini into strips lengthwise. Place strips between paper towels to absorb moisture. Set aside.
2. In a medium saucepan over medium heat, melt butter. Add onion and saute until fragrant. Add garlic and saute for 30 seconds.
3. Pour in the coconut cream, broth and xanthan gum. Turn off heat and whisk until it begins to thicken, about 3 minutes.
4. In a medium bowl, add Ricotta cheese. salt, garlic powder and oregano, then mix well. Fold in spinach, mushrooms and ½ cup Mozzarella cheese.
5. Pour half of the sauce into a round baking pan.
6. To assemble the rolls, place two strips of zucchini on a work surface. Spoon 2 tablespoons of Ricotta mixture onto the slices and roll up. Place seam side down on top of sauce. Repeat with remaining ingredients.
7. Pour the remaining sauce over the rolls and sprinkle with remaining Mozzarella cheese. Cover with foil and place into the air fryer basket.
8. Adjust the temperature to 350 F (177 C) and bake for 20 minutes.
9. In the last 5 minutes, remove the foil to brown the cheese. Serve immediately. Enjoy!

Vegetarian Parmesan Artichokes

Prep Time: 10 Minutes | **Cooking Time:** 10 Minutes | **Servings:** 4 | **Calories:** 189 | **Fat:** 13 g | **Protein:** 8 g | **Carbs:** 6 g | **Fiber:** 4 g

Ingredients and Quantity

- 2 medium artichokes, trimmeed and quartered, center removed
- 2 tbsp. coconut oil
- ¼ cup flax egg
- ¼ cup blanched finely ground almond flour
- ½ cup grated vegetarian Parmesan cheese
- ½ tsp. crushed red pepper flakes

Direction

1. In a large bowl, toss artichokes in coconut oil and then dip each piece into the flax egg.
2. Mix the Permesan cheese and almond flour in a large bowl. Add artichoke pieces and toss to cover as completely as possible. Sprinkle with pepper flakes.
3. Place into the air fryer basket. Adjust the temperature to 400 F (205 C) and air fry for 10 minutes.
4. Toss the basket two times during cooking. Serve warm. Enjoy!

Zucchini Cauliflower Cheese Fritters

Prep Time: 15 Minutes | **Cooking Time:** 12 Minutes | **Servings:** 2 | **Calories:** 217 | **Fat:** 12 g | **Protein:** 14 g | **Carbs:** 8 g | **Fiber:** 8 g

Ingredients and Quantity

- 1 (12 oz. or 340 g) steamer bag cauliflower
- 1 medium-size zucchini, shredded
- ¼ cup almond flour
- ¼ cup applesauce
- ½ tsp. garlic powder
- ¼ cup grated vegetarian Parmesan cheese

Direction

1. Cook cauliflower according to package instructions and drain excess moisture in cheesecloth or paper towel. Place into a large bowl.
2. Place the zucchini into paper towel and pat down to remove excess moisture. Add to bowl with cauliflower. Then add the remaining ingredients, mix to combine.
3. Divide the mixture evenly and form four patties. Press into ½-inch thick patties. Then place each patties into the air fryer basket.
4. Adjust the temperature to 320 F (160 C) and air fry for 12 minutes.
5. Fritters will be firm when fully cooked. Alow to cool for 5 minutes before transferring to serving plate. Serve warm. Enjoy!

Spaghetti Squash with Alfredo Sauce

Prep Time: 10 Minutes | **Cooking Time:** 15 Minutes | **Servings:** 2 | **Calories:** 375 | **Fat:** 24 g | **Protein:** 13 g | **Carbs:** 16 g | **Fiber:** 4 g

Ingredients and Quantity

- ½ large cooked spaghetti squash
- 2 tbsp. salted almond butter, melted
- ½ cup low carb Alfredo sauce
- ¼ cup grated vegetarian Parmesan cheese
- ½ tsp. garlic powder
- 1 tsp. dried parsley
- ¼ tsp. ground peppercorn
- ½ cup shredded Italian blend cheese

Direction

1. Using a fork, remove the strands of spaghetti squash from the shell. Place into a large bowl with Alfredo sauce. Sprinkle with garlic powder, parsley and peppercorn.
2. Pour into a 4-cup round baking dish and top with shredded cheese. Place the dish into the air fryer basket.
3. Adjust the temperature to 320 F (160 C) and bake for 15 minutes.
4. When done, cheese will be golden and bubbling. Serve immediately. Enjoy!

Caprese Eggplant Stacks with Basil

Prep Time: 5 Minutes | **Cooking Time:** 12 Minutes | **Servings:** 4 | **Calories:** 195 | **Fat:** 13 g | **Protein:** 8 g | **Carbs:** 8 g | **Fiber:** 5 g

Ingredients and Quantity

- 1 mediu-size eggplant, cut into ¼ inch slices
- 2 large tomatoes, cut into ¼ inch slices
- 4 oz. (113 g) fresh Mozzarella cheese, cut into ½ oz or 14 g slices
- 2 tbsp. olive oil
- ¼ cup fresh basil, sliced

Direction

1. In a baking dish, place four slices of eggplant on the bottom. Place a slice of tomato on top of each eggplant round, then Mozzarella, then eggplant. Repeat as necessary.
2. Drizzle with olive oil. Cover dish with foil and place dish into the air fryer basket.
3. Adjust the temperature to 350 F (180 C) and bake for 12 minutes.
4. When done, the eggplant will be tender. Garnish with fresh basil to serve. Enjoy!

Crustless Cheddar Spinach Pie

Prep Time: 10 Minutes | **Cooking Time:** 20 Minutes | **Servings:** 4 | **Calories:** 288 | **Fat:** 20 g | **Protein:** 18 g | **Carbs:** 2 g | **Fiber:** 2 g

Ingredients and Quantity

- 1 ½ cups applesauce
- ¼ cup coconut cream
- 1 cup frozen chopped spinach, drained
- 1 cup shredded sharp Cheddar cheese
- ¼ cup diced yellow onion

Direction

1. In a medium bowl, pour the applesauce and ccoconut cream, then mix well. Now add the remaining ingredients to the bowl and mix well.
2. Pour into a round baking dish. Then place into the air fryer basket.
3. Adjust the temperature to 320 F (160 C) and bake for 20 minutes.
4. The pie will be firm and slightly browned when fully cooked. Serve immediately. Enjoy!

Broccoli Cheese Crust Pizza

Prep Time: 15 Minutes | **Cooking Time:** 12 Minutes | **Servings:** 4 | **Calories:** 136 | **Fat:** 7 g | **Protein:** 10 g | **Carbs:** 4 g | **Fiber:** 2 g

Ingredients and Quantity

- 3 cups riced broccoli, steamed and drained well
- ¼ cup applesauce
- ½ cup grated vegetarian Parmesan cheese
- 3 tbsp. low carb Alfredo sauce
- ½ cup shredded vegan Mozzarella cheese

Direction

1. In a large bowl, mix the broccoli, applesauce and Parmesan cheese.
2. Cut a piece of parchment to fit your air fryer basket. Press out the pizza to fit on the parchment, working in two batches if necessary. Then place into the air fryer basket.
3. Adjust the temperature to 370 F (188 C) and air fry for 5 minutes.

4. The crust should be firm enough to flip. If not, air for additional 2 minutes. Then flip the crust.
5. Top with Alfredo sauce and Mozzarella cheese. Return to the air fryer basket and cook an additional 7 minutes or until cheese is golden and bubbling. Serve warm. Enjoy!

Mini Sweet Pepper Nachos

Prep Time: 10 Minutes | **Cooking Time:** 5 Minutes | **Servings:** 2 | **Calories:** 310 | **Fat:** 23 g | **Protein:** 12 g | **Carbs:** 6 g | **Fiber:** 5 g

Ingredients and Quantity

- 6 mini sweet peppers, seeded and sliced in half
- ¾ cup shredded Violife cheese
- ¼ cup sliced pickled jalapenos
- ½ medium-size avocado, peeled, pitted and diced
- 2 tbsp. full-fat coconut milk

Direction

1. Place the peppers into an ungreased, round, non-stick baking dish. Sprinkle with Violife cheese and top with jalapenos.
2. Place dish into air fryer basket. Adjust temperature to 350 F (180 C) and bake for 5 minutes. Cheese will be melted and bubbly when done.
3. Remove dish from air fryer and top with avocado. Drizzle with coconut milk. Serve warm. Enjoy!

Cauliflower Rice-Stuffed Bell Peppers

Prep Time: 10 Minutes | **Cooking Time:** 5 Minutes | **Servings:** 2 | **Calories:** 310 | **Fat:** 23 g | **Protein:** 12 g | **Carbs:** 6 g | **Fiber:** 5 g

Ingredients and Quantity

- 2 cups uncooked cauliflower rice
- ¼ cup drained petite diced tomatoes
- 2 tbsp. olive oil
- 1 cup shredded vegan Mozzarella cheese
- ¼ tsp. salt
- ¼ tsp. ground black pepper
- 4 medium-size green bell peppers, tops removed, seeded

Direction

1. In a large bowl, mix all the ingredients except the bell pepper.
2. Remove the seeds and flesh of the bell peppers to make enough room for the stuffing.
3. Scoop the mixture evenly into the peppers.
4. Place the peppers into ungreased air fryer basket. Adjust the temperature to 350 F (180 C) and air fry for 15 minutes.
5. Peppers will be tender and cheese will melt when done. Serve warm. Enjoy!

Mushroom and Zucchini Burgers

Prep Time: 10 Minutes | **Cooking Time:** 12 Minutes | **Servings:** 4 | **Calories:** 48 | **Fat:** 2 g | **Protein:** 3 g | **Carbs:** 4 g | **Fiber:** 1 g

Ingredients and Quantity

- 8 oz. (227 g) Cremini mushrooms
- 2/4 cup applesauce
- ½ medium-size zucchini, trimmed and chopped
- ¼ cup peeled and chopped yellow onion
- 1 garlic clove, peeled and finely minced
- ½ tsp. salt
- ¼ tsp. ground black pepper

Direction

1. Place all the ingredients into a food processor and pulse twenty times, until finely chopped and combined.
2. Divide and separate the mixture into four equal sections and press each section into a burger shape.
3. Place the burgers into ungreased air fryer basket.
4. Adjust the temperature to 375 F (190 C) and air fry for 12 minutes, turning burgers halfway through cooking time. Burgers will be browned and firm when done.
5. Place the burgers on a large plate and cool for 5 minutes before serving. Enjoy!

Basil Pesto Spinach Flatbread

Prep Time: 10 Minutes | **Cooking Time:** 8 Minutes | **Servings:** 4 | **Calories:** 414 | **Fat:** 31 g | **Protein:** 21 g | **Carbs:** 7 g | **Fiber:** 3 g

Ingredients and Quantity

- 1 cup blanched finely ground almond flour
- 2 oz. (57 g) vegan cream cheese
- 2 cups shredded Mozzarella cheese
- 1 cup chopped fresh spinach leaves
- 2 tbsp. basil pesto

Direction

1. Place flour, cream cheese and Mozzarella cheese in a large microwave-safe bowl and microwave on High for 45 seconds, then stir.
2. Fold in the spinach and microwave an additional 15 seconds. Stir until a soft dough ball forms.
3. Cut two pieces of parchment papers to fit the air air fryer basket.
4. Separate dough into two sections and press each out on ungreased parchment to create 6-inch rounds.
5. Spread 1 tablwspoon pesto over each flatbread and place rounds on parchment into ungreased air fryer basket.
6. Adjust the temperature to 350 F (180 C) and air fry for 8 minutes, turning crusts halfway through cooking. Flatbread will be golden when done.
7. Allow to cool for 5 minutes before slicing and serving. Enjoy!

Green Cabbage Steaks

Prep Time: 5 Minutes | **Cooking Time:** 10 Minutes | **Servings:** 4 | **Calories:** 105 | **Fat:** 7 g | **Protein:** 2 g | **Carbs:** 6 g | **Fiber:** 5 g

Ingredients and Quantity

- 1 small head green cabbage, cored and cut into ½-inch slices
- ¼ tsp. salt
- ¼ tsp. ground black pepper
- 2 tbsp. olive oil
- 1 garlic clove, peeled and finely minced
- ½ tsp. dried thyme
- ½ tsp. dried parsley

Direction

1. Sprinkle each side of cabbage with salt and pepper, then place into ungreased air fryer basket, working in batch if necessary.
2. Drizzle each side of cabbage with olive oil, then sprinkle with remaining ingredients on both sides.
3. Adjust the temperature to 350 F (180 C) and air fry for 10 minutes, turning "steaks" halfway through cooking.
4. Cabbage will be browned at the edge and tender when done. Serve warm. Enjoy!

Brussels Sprouts with Toasted Pecan

Prep Time: 10 Minutes | **Cooking Time:** 30 Minutes | **Servings:** 4 | **Calories:** 250 | **Fat:** 19 g | **Protein:** 9 g | **Carbs:** 9 g | **Fiber:** 8 g

Ingredients and Quantity

- ½ cup pecans
- 1 ½ pounds (680 g) fresh Brussels sprouts, trimmed and quartered
- 2 tbsp. olive oil
- Salt and freshly ground black pepper
- ¼ cup crumbled vegan Gorgonzola cheese

Direction

1. Spread the pecans in a single layer in the air fryer basket. Set the temperature to 350 F (180 C) and air fry for 3 to 5 minutes until the pecans are lightly browned and fragrant.
2. Transfer the pecans to a plate and continue prheating the air fryer, increasing the temperature to 400 F (205 C).
3. In a large bowl, toss the Brussels sprouts with the olive oil and season with salt and black pepper to taste.
4. Working in batches if necessary, arrange the Brussels sprouts in a single layer in the air fryer. Pausing halfway through the cooking time to shake the air fryer basket, air fry for 20 to 25 minutes, until the sprouts are tender and starting to brown on the edges.
5. Transfer the sprouts to a serving bowl and top with the toasted pecans and Gorgonzola cheese. Serve warm or at room temperature. Enjoy!

Jenny Crawford

LOW CARB PLANT BASED VEGAN AND VEGETARIAN AIR FRYER RECIPES FOR WEIGHT WATCHERS

Appetizer, Breakfast and Snack Recipes

Broccoli Quiche

Prep Time: 10 Minutes | **Cooking Time:** 10 Minutes | **Servings:** 1 | **Calories:** 656 | **Fat:** 19 g | **Carbs:** 18 g | **Protein:** 21 g

Ingredients and Quantity

- ¼ cup flax egg
- 60 ml coconut cream
- 5 tiny broccoli florets
- 1 tbsp. grated vegan cheddar cheese

Direction

1. Preheat your air fryer to 162 C (325 F).
2. Mix the flax egg with the coconut cream and cheese in a bowl.
3. Fold in the broccoli and mix evenly.
4. Add this mixture to a suitable-sized pan.
5. Transfer the pan to the air fryer basket.
6. Air fry the quiche for 10 minutes in the preheated air fryer. Serve and enjoy!

Breakfast Sandwich

Prep Time: 10 Minutes | **Cooking Time:** 20 Minutes | **Servings:** 2 | **Calories:** 346 | **Fat:** 13.9 g | **Carbs:** 33.1 g | **Protein:** 20.9 g

Ingredients and Quantity

- 2 bagels, sliced
- ½ tsp. canola oil
- 4 super firm tofu, cut into ¼ inch thick
- ¼ tsp. salt
- ¼ tsp. nutritional yeast flakes
- ¼ tsp. granulated onion
- 1 pinch black pepper
- 2 tbsp. vegan cream cheese

Direction

1. Preheat your air fryer to 200 C (390 F).
2. Cut the bagel in halves and toast them in a frying pan until golden brown.
3. Place the breakfast sausages in the air fryer basket.
4. Air fry the sausages for 10 minutes in the preheated air fryer.
5. Flip the vegan sausages once cooked halfway through.
6. Sear the sliced tofu with oil in a frying pan for 3 to 5 minutes per side.
7. Stir in salt, yeast, onion flakes and black pepper.
8. Spread the cream cheese inside the bagels.
9. Add tofu to the bagels. Serve and enjoy!

Banana Bread

Prep Time: 10 Minutes | **Cooking Time:** 28 Minutes | **Servings:** 6 | **Calories:** 305 | **Fat:** 25 g | **Carbs:** 2.3 g | **Protein:** 18.3 g

Ingredients and Quantity

- 100 g all-purpose flour
- ¼ tsp. baking soda
- ¼ tsp. salt
- ¼ cup flax egg
- 2 bananas overriped, mashed
- ½ tsp. vanilla
- 60 ml full-fat coconut milk
- 59 ml vegetable oil
- 100 g sugar

Direction

1. Mash bananas in a suitable bowl and add vanilla, sour cream, vegetable oil, and egg.
2. Beat these ingredients until well incorporated.
3. Stir in all-purpose flour, sugar, baking soda, and salt.
4. Mix well to get a smooth and thick batter.
5. Pour this batter into a greased 7 inches Bundt pan.
6. Place this Bundt pan in the Air Fryer basket.
7. Return the Air Fryer basket to the Air Fryer.
8. Air Fry at 150 C (300 F) for 28 minutes.
9. Once done, remove the basket and the pan from the Air Fryer.
10. Transfer the prepared bread to a wire rack and allow it to cool.
11. Slice and serve. Enjoy!

Pepperoni Crisps

Prep Time: 10 Minutes | **Cooking Time:** 8 Minutes | **Servings:** 5 | **Calories:** 100 | **Fat:** 2 g | **Carbs:** 4 g | **Protein:** 18 g

Ingredients and Quantity

- 10 pepperoni slices

Direction

1. Spread the pepperoni in the air fryer basket in a single layer.
2. Return the air fryer basket to the air fryer.
3. Air fry at 180 C (350 F) for 8 minutes.
4. Toss and flip the fries in the basket once cooked halfway through.
5. Return the basket and resume the cooking. Serve warm. Enjoy!

Ranch Chickpeas

Prep Time: 10 Minutes | **Cooking Time:** 8 Minutes | **Servings:** 6 | **Calories:** 186 | **Fat:** 3 g | **Carbs:** 31 g | **Protein:** 9.7 g

Ingredients and Quantity

- 1 tbsp. dry ranch dressing
- 1 can (425 g) chickpeas, drained
- 2 tbsp. vegan-friendly sauce

Direction

1. Preheat the air fryer to 180 C (350 F).
2. Drain the canned chickpeas and spread them on a baking sheet lined with a paper towel.
3. Toss the chickpeas with the vegan sauce and ranch dressing powder in a bowl.
4. Spread the chickpeas in the air fryer basket.
5. Return the air fryer basket to the air fryer and cook for 8 minutes at 180 C (350 F).
6. Toss the chickpeas once cooked halfway through. Serve warm. Enjoy!

Tofu Rancheros

Prep Time: 15 Minutes | **Cooking Time:** 16 Minutes | **Servings:** 4 | **Calories:** 457 | **Fat:** 3.6 g | **Carbs:** 82.5 g | **Protein:** 27.5 g

Ingredients and Quantity

- 1 container (556 g) tofu, cut into cubes
- 1 tsp. ground cumin powder
- 1 tsp. ground chilli powder
- ½ tsp. smoked paprika
- ¼ tsp. salt, or to taste

For the Salsa Beans:

- 1 can (439 g) black beans, drained
- 59 g mild salsa
- 1/8 tsp. liquid smoke
- 1/8 tsp. jalapeno powder
- 1/8 tsp. cumin powder
- Salt, to taste

For Veggie Topping:

- 30 g carrot, grated
- 25 g Courgette, grated
- 40 g yellow squash, grated
- 1/8 tsp. salt
- 1 pinch black pepper

For Base:

- 4 large flour tortillas
- 120 g vegan cheese, shredded

Direction

1. Mix tofu with salt, paprika, chilli powder and cumin in a bowl.
2. Preheat the air fryer to 200 C (390 F).
3. Add the prepared tofu to the air fryer basket and air fry for 10 minutes at 200 C (390 F).
4. Shake the tofu once cooked halfway through.
5. Mix all the recipes ingredients for the salsa beans in a suitable bowl.
6. Spread the tortillas in a flat pan and sear for 2 to 3 minutes per side.
7. Top each tortillas with ¼ vgean cheese, ¼ salsa beans, ¼ tofu and shredded veggies.
8. Add a spoonful of mild salsa on top. Serve and enjoy!

Battered Fried Tofu

Prep Time: 10 Minutes | **Cooking Time:** 10 Minutes | **Servings:** 6 | **Calories:** 297 | **Fat:** 2.8 g | **Carbs:** 54.4 g | **Protein:** 9.5 g

Ingredients and Quantity

For the Tofu:

- 227 g block of firm tofu, cut into 4 sliced
- ½ tsp. black pepper
- 1 tsp. salt

Dry Ingredients:

- 180 g all-purpose flour
- 42 g corn flour
- 1 tbsp. garlic powder
- 1 tbsp. onion powder
- 1 tbsp. salt
- 1 tbsp. paprika
- 2 tsp. cayenne

Wet Ingredients:

- 236 ml soy milk
- 2 tsp. apple cider vinegar
- 2 tbsp. vegan egg powder
- 118 ml ice-cold water
- 2 tbsp. bourbon

- 1 tbsp. hot sauce
- Non-stick oil spray

Direction

1. Preheat the air fryer to 200 C (390 F).
2. Mix bourbon with hot sauce, egg powder, water, vinegar and soy milk in a bowl.
3. Stir in the flour, garlic powder and all the dry ingredients.
4. Mix well until smooth, then toss in the tofu.
5. Place the coated tofu in the air fryer basket and air fry for 10 minutes at 200 C (390 F).
6. Flip the tofu once cooked halfway through. Serve and enjoy!

Crunch Wrap

Prep Time: 10 Minutes | **Cooking Time:** 12 Minutes | **Servings:** 2 | **Calories:** 264 | **Fat:** 13.9 g | **Carbs:** 29.5 g | **Protein:** 8 g

Ingredients and Quantity

- 1 regular gluten-free tortilla
- 2 tbsp. refried pinto beans
- 2 tbsp. grated vegan cheese
- 1 small corn tortilla
- 3 iceberg lettuce leaves
- 2 tbsp. guacamole
- 3 tbsp. salsa

Direction

1. Preheat the air fryer to 160 C (325 F).
2. Spread the tortilla and top it with beans, cheese, salsa, corn and the rest of the ingredients.
3. Roll this tortilla neatly and place it in the air fryer basket.
4. Air fry this wrap for 6 minutes in the preheated air fryer. Serve and enjoy!

Reuben Rolls

Prep Time: 10 Minutes | **Cooking Time:** 13 Minutes | **Servings:** 6 | **Calories:** 208 | **Fat:** 5.5 g | **Carbs:** 38.9 g | **Protein:** 4.2 g

Ingredients and Quantity

- 1 can (567 g) jackfruit, drained
- 78 ml Vegan Thousand Island Dressing
- 1 small sweet onion, peeled and minced
- 6 vegan cheese slices
- 2 dill pickles, chopped
- 12 vegan wonton wrappers

Direction

1. Shred jackfruit with a fork and mix it with island dressing in a bowl.
2. Cover and marinate the jackfruit for 15 minutes.
3. Sauté garlic and onion with oil in a suitable saucepan for 5 minutes.
4. Remove this mixture from the heat and stir in the jackfruit mixture.
5. Spread a wonton wrapper in a diamond shape and add 2 tablespoons jackfruit mixture on the bottom corner.
6. Add ½ slice of cheese and 1 tablespoon pickles on top.
7. Roll the wrapper starting from the bottom.
8. Make more rolls in the same manner and brush each roll with pickle juice.
9. Preheat your air fryer to 180 C (350 F).

10. Place the rolls in the air fryer basket and air fry for 8 minutes at 180 C (350 F).
11. Flip the rolls once cooked halfway through and resume cooking. Serve warm. Enjoy!

Crostini with Hummus

Prep Time: 10 Minutes | **Cooking Time:** 4 Minutes | **Servings:** 4 | **Calories:** 273 | **Fat:** 14.9 g | **Carbs:** 28.7 g | **Protein:** 10.3 g

Ingredients and Quantity

For the Marinated Cashews:

- 70 g raw cashews
- 1 tbsp. olive oil
- 1 tbsp. lemon juice
- 1 tsp. balsamic vinegar
- ½ tsp. dried basil
- ½ tsp. dried oregano
- 1/8 tsp. granulated onion
- 1 garlic clove, minced
- Pinch salt

For the Crostini:

- 1 baguette cut into ½ inch slices
- Olive oil for toasting the crostini
- 280 g hummus
- 170 g grilled artichoke hearts from the oil-packed jars, drained and sliced

Direction

1. Blend the cashews with a pinch of salt, garlic, onion, oregano, basil, vinegar, oil and lemon juice in a quality blender until smooth.
2. Preheat the air fryer to 190 C (375 F).
3. Place the baguette slices in the air fryer basket.
4. Air fry for 4 minutes in the preheated air fryer.
5. Spread the hummus over the baguette slices.
6. Divide the cashew mixture and grilled artichokes on top. Serve and enjoy!

Popcorn Tofu Nuggets

Prep Time: 15 Minutes | **Cooking Time:** 12 Minutes | **Servings:** 6 | **Calories:** 392 | **Fat:** 8.7 g | **Carbs:** 59.3 g | **Protein:** 21.1 g

Ingredients and Quantity

- 400 g tofu, drained and pressed
- 60 g quinoa flour
- 60 g cornmeal
- 3 tbsp. nutritional yeast
- 2 tbsp. Bouillon, vegetarian
- 1 tbsp. Dijon mustard
- 2 tsp. garlic powder
- 2 tsp. onion powder
- ½ tsp. salt
- ½ tsp. pepper
- 177 ml almond milk
- 180 g panko breadcrumbs

Direction

1. Preheat the air fryer to 180 C (350 F).
2. Mix the flour with milk, pepper, salt, onion, garlic, mustard and bouillon in a bowl until smooth.
3. Dip the tofu in the batter and coat the panko breadcrumbs.
4. Place the coated tofu in the air fryer basket, then air fry for 12 minutes at 180 C (350 F).
5. Flip the tofu nuggets once cooked halfway through. Serve and enjoy!

Onion Rings

Prep Time: 15 Minutes | **Cooking Time:** 15 Minutes | **Servings:** 6 | **Calories:** 139 | **Fat:** 1.4 g | **Carbs:** 27.1 g | **Protein:** 4.2 g

Ingredients and Quantity

- 3 yellow onions

Wet Ingredients:

- 120 g flour
- 158 ml almond milk
- ½ tsp. paprika
- ¼ tsp. turmeric
- ½ tsp. salt

Dry Ingredients:

- 150 g panko breadcrumbs
- ½ tsp. paprika
- ¼ tsp. turmeric
- ¼ tsp. salt

Direction

1. Preheat the air fryer to 200 C (390 F).
2. Mix flour with milk, paprika, turmeric and salt in a bowl, until smooth.
3. Toss breadcrumbs with salt, turmeric and paprika in a bowl.
4. Cut the onions into ½ inch thick slices and separate them into rings.
5. Dip each ring in the flour batter and coat with panko crumbs
6. Place the prepared onion rings in the air fryer basket and air fry for 15 minutes at 200 C (390 F).
7. Flip the onion rings once cooked halfway through, then resume cooking. Serve and enjoy!

Potato Nuggets

Prep Time: 10 Minutes | **Cooking Time:** 19 Minutes | **Servings:** 6 | **Calories:** 113 | **Fat:** 3 g | **Carbs:** 19.5 g | **Protein:** 3.5 g

Ingredients and Quantity

- 269 g chopped potatoes
- 1 tsp. olive oil
- 1 garlic clove, minced
- 268 g chopped kale
- 29 ml almond milk
- ¼ tsp. sea salt
- 1/8 tsp. ground black pepper
- Vegetable oil spray, as needed

Direction

1. Add potatoes to a saucepan filled with boiling water and cook for 30 minutes until soft.
2. Sauté garlic with oil in a frying pan for 30 seconds until golden brown.
3. Stir in kale and cook for 3 minutes, then transfer it to a bowl.
4. Drain the cooked potatoes and allow them to cool.
5. Mash the cooked potatoes in a bowl with a potato masher.
6. Stir in kale, black pepper, milk, and salt, then mix well.
7. Preheat the Air fry to 200 C (390 F).
8. Make 1-inch balls out of this potato mixture and place them in the air fryer basket.
9. Spray the potato nuggets with vegetable oil and air fry them for 15 minutes at 200 C (390 F).
10. Flip the balls once cooked halfway through. Serve and enjoy!

Main Meal Recipes

Air Fried Fajitas

Prep Time: 10 Minutes | **Cooking Time:** 15 Minutes | **Servings:** 2 | **Calories:** 255 | **Fat:** 13.8 g | **Carbs:** 27.2 g | **Protein:** 3.2 g

Ingredients and Quantity

- 88 g mushrooms, sliced
- 1 red capsicum sliced into ½ inch slices
- 1 yellow capsicum sliced into ½ inch slices
- 1 green capsicum sliced into ½ inch slices
- 1 red onion, sliced into wedges
- 3 tbsp. vegan fajita seasoning (I used McCormick)
- 1 tbsp. vegetable oil

Direction

1. Toss mushrooms with peppers, onion fajita seasoning and oil in a bowl.
2. Spread the fajita mixture in the Air Fryer basket.
3. Spray them with cooking spray.
4. Return the Air Fryer basket to the Air Fryer.
5. Air fry these veggies for 15 minutes at 200 C (390 F). Serve warm. Enjoy!

Black Bean Burger

Prep Time: 10 Minutes | **Cooking Time:** 15 Minutes | **Servings:** 6 | **Calories:** 350 | **Fat:** 2.6 g | **Carbs:** 64.6 g | **Protein:** 19.9 g

Ingredients and Quantity

- 110 g rolled oats
- 454 g canned black bean
- 200 g salsa
- 1 tbsp. soy sauce
- 1 ¼ tsp. mild chili powder
- ¼ to ½ tsp. chipotle chili powder
- ½ tsp. garlic powder
- 76 g corn kernels

Direction

1. Add all the rolled oats to a food processor and pulse to get a coarse meal.
2. Add black beans, salsa, soy sauce, chili powder, Chile powder, and garlic powder.
3. Blend again for 1 minute, then transfer to a bowl.
4. Stir in corn kernel, then make six patties out of this mixture.
5. Place the black bean patties in the Air Fryer basket.
6. Return the Air Fryer basket to the Air Fryer.
7. Air Fry at 190 C (375 F) for 15 minutes.
8. Flip the patties once cooked halfway through and resume cooking. Serve warm. Enjoy!

Potato Cakes

Prep Time: 15 Minutes | **Cooking Time:** 10 Minutes | **Servings:** 4 | **Calories:** 208 | **Fat:** 5 g | **Carbs:** 34.1 g | **Protein:** 5.9 g

Ingredients and Quantity

- 558 g potatoes, sliced
- 1 bunch green onions, chopped
- 1 lime, zest and juice
- 1 ½ inch knob fresh ginger
- 1 tbsp. tamari
- 4 tbsp. red curry paste
- 4 sheets nori, chopped
- 1 can heart of palm, drained
- 250 g canned artichoke hearts, drained
- Black pepper, to taste
- Salt, to taste

Direction

1. Add potato cubes to a pot filled with water.
2. Place it over medium heat and cook until potatoes are soft.
3. Drain the cooked potatoes and transfer them to a suitable bowl.
4. Mash the potatoes with a masher, then add green onions, lime juice, and remaining ingredients.
5. Mix well and stir in artichoke shreds.
6. Stir well and make 4 patties out of this mixture.
7. Place the patties in the Air Fryer basket.
8. Return the Air Fryer basket to the Air Fryer.
9. Air Fry at 190 C (375 F) for 10 minutes.
10. Flip the patties once cooked halfway through and resume cooking. Serve warm. Enjoy!

Parmesan Aubergine

Prep Time: 10 Minutes | **Cooking Time:** 15 Minutes | **Servings:** 4 | **Calories:** 231 | **Fat:** 9 g | **Carbs:** 32.1 g | **Protein:** 6.3 g

Ingredients and Quantity

- 60 g flour
- 118 ml almond milk
- 70 g panko breadcrumbs
- 2 tbsp. parmesan, grated
- Onion powder, to taste
- Garlic powder, to taste
- 1 large aubergine, stems removed and sliced
- Salt and black pepper, to taste

Aubergine Parmesan:

- 225 g marinara sauce
- 112 g vegan Mozarella shreds
- Vegan Parmesan, grated

Direction

1. Mix panko crumbs with garlic powder, black pepper, salt, onion powder, and vegan parmesan in a bowl.
2. First coat the aubergine slices with flour, then dip in the almond milk and finally coat with breadcrumbs mixture.
3. Place the coated aubergine slices in the Air Fryer basket.
4. Return the Air Fryer basket to the Air Fryer.
5. Air Fry at 200 C (390 F) for 15 minutes.
6. Flip the aubergine slices once cooked halfway through.
7. Place the aubergine slices on the serving plate and top them with marinara sauce and cheese. Serve warm. Enjoy!

Veggie Bites

Prep Time: 10 Minutes | **Cooking Time:** 10 Minutes | **Servings:** 4 | **Calories:** 270 | **Fat:** 14.6 g | **Carbs:** 31.3 g | **Protein:** 6.4 g

Ingredients and Quantity

- 1 large broccoli, cut into florets
- 6 large carrots, diced
- Handful of garden peas

- ½ cauliflower, riced
- 1 large onion, peeled and diced
- 1 small Courgette, diced
- 2 leeks, sliced
- 236 ml coconut milk
- 57 g plain flour
- 1 cm cube ginger peeled and grated
- 1 tbsp. garlic puree
- 1 tbsp. olive oil
- 1 tbsp. Thai green curry paste
- 1 tbsp. coriander
- 1 tbsp. mixed spice
- 1 tsp. cumin
- Salt and black pepper, to taste

Direction

1. Place leek and Courgette in a steamer basket and steam them for 20 minutes.
2. Sauté onion, ginger, and garlic with olive oil in a frying pan until soft.
3. Add steamed leek and Courgette to the frying pan and sauté for 5 minutes.
4. Stir in coconut milk and the rest of the spices.
5. Mix well, then add the cauliflower rice then cook for 10 minutes.
6. Remove the hot frying pan from the heat and allow it to cool.
7. Cover and refrigerate this mixture for 1 hour.
8. Slice the mixture into bite-sized pieces and place these pieces in the Air Fryer basket.
9. Return the Air Fryer basket to the Air Fryer.
10. Air Fry at 180 C (350 F) for 10 minutes.
11. Carefully flip the bites once cooked halfway through, then resume cooking. Serve warm. Enjoy!

Air Fried Falafel

Prep Time: 15 Minutes | **Cooking Time:** 10 Minutes | **Servings:** 6 | **Calories:** 206 | **Fat:** 3.4 g | **Carbs:** 35 g | **Protein:** 10.6 g

Ingredients and Quantity

- 320 g dry garbanzo beans
- 20 g fresh parsley, chopped
- 20 g fresh coriander, chopped
- 57 g white onion, chopped
- 7 garlic cloves, minced
- 2 tbsp. all-purpose flour
- ½ tsp. sea salt
- 1 tbsp. ground cumin
- 1/8 tsp. ground cardamom
- 1 tsp. ground cayenne pepper

Direction

1. Soak garbanzo beans in a bowl filled with water for 24 hours.
2. Drain and transfer the beans to a cooking pot filled with water.
3. Cook the beans for 1 hour or more on simmer until soft.
4. Add coriander, onion, garlic, and parsley to a food processor and blend until finely chopped.
5. Drain the cooked garbanzo beans and transfer them to the food processor.
6. Add salt, cardamom, cayenne, coriander, cumin, and flour.
7. Blend until it makes a rough dough.
8. Transfer this falafel mixture to a bowl, cover with a plastic wrap and refrigerate for 2 hours.
9. Make 1 ½ inches balls out of this bean's mixture.
10. Lightly press the balls and place them in the Air Fryer basket.
11. Return the Air Fryer basket to the Air Fryer.
12. Air Fry at 200 C (390 F) for 10 minutes.
13. Flip the falafels once cooked halfway through the resume cooking. Serve warm. Enjoy!

Saucy Carrots

Prep Time: 10 Minutes | **Cooking Time:** 25 Minutes | **Servings:** 4 | **Calories:** 206 | **Fat:** 3.4 g | **Carbs:** 35 g | **Protein:** 10.6 g

Ingredients and Quantity

- 450 g carrots, cut into chunks
- 1 tbsp. sesame oil
- ½ tbsp. ginger, minced
- ½ tbsp. soy sauce
- ½ tsp. garlic, minced
- ½ tbsp. scallions, chopped, for garnishing
- ½ tsp. sesame seeds, for garnishing

Direction

1. Preheat the air fryer to 200 C (390 F).
2. Toss all the ginger carrots ingredients, except the sesame seeds and scallions, in a suitable bowl.
3. Place the seasoned carrots in the air fryer basket in a single layer.
4. Return the air fryer basket to the air fryer and cook for 25 minutes at 200 C (390 F).
5. Toss the carrots once cooked halfway through.
6. Garnish with the sesame seeds and scallions. Serve warm. Enjoy!

Potato Tater Tots

Prep Time: 10 Minutes | **Cooking Time:** 27 Minutes | **Servings:** 4 | **Calories:** 185 | **Fat:** 11 g | **Carbs:** 21 g | **Protein:** 4.7 g

Ingredients and Quantity

- 2 potatoes, peeled
- ½ tsp. vegan Cajun seasoning (I used McCormick)
- Olive oil cooking spray
- Sea salt, to taste

Direction

1. Preheat the air fryer to 190 C (375 F).
2. Boil water in a cooking pot and cook the potatoes in it for 15 minutes at 190 C (375 F).
3. Drain and leave the potatoes to cool in a bowl.
4. Grate these potatoes and toss them with Cajun seasoning.
5. Make small tater tots out of this mixture.
6. Place these tots in the air fryer basket and spray them with cooking oil.
7. Return the air fryer basket to the air fryer and cook for 27 minutes at 190 C (375 F).
8. Flip them once cooked halfway through, and resume cooking. Serve warm. Enjoy!

Cauliflower Gnocchi

Prep Time: 10 Minutes | **Cooking Time:** 17 Minutes | **Servings:** 4 | **Calories:** 134 | **Fat:** 5.9 g | **Carbs:** 9.5 g | **Protein:** 10.4 g

Ingredients and Quantity

- 1 bag frozen cauliflower gnocchi
- 1 ½ tbsp. olive oil
- 1 tsp. garlic powder
- 3 tbsp. vegan Parmesan, grated

- ½ tsp. dried basil
- Fresh parsley, chopped, for topping

Direction

1. Preheat your air fryer to 200 C (390 F).
2. Toss the gnocchi with olive oil, garlic powder, 1 tablespoon parmesan, salt and basil in a bowl.
3. Place the cauliflower gnocchi in the air fryer basket.
4. Return the air fryer basket to the air fryer and cook for 10 minutes at 200 C (390 F).
5. Toss the gnocchi once cooked halfway through, then resume cooking.
6. Drizzle the remaining Parmesan on top of the gnochi and cook again for 7 minutes. Serve warm. Enjoy!

Peppered Asparagus

Prep Time: 10 Minutes | **Cooking Time:** 16 Minutes | **Servings:** 4 | **Calories:** 163 | **Fat:** 11.5 g | **Carbs:** 8.3 g | **Protein:** 7.4 g

Ingredients and Quantity

- 1 bunch asparagus, trimmed
- Avocado or olive oil
- Himalayan salt, to taste
- Black pepper, to taste

Direction

1. Preheat the air fryer to 200 C (390 F).
2. Place the trimmed asparagus in the air fryer basket.
3. Top the asparagus with salt, black pepper and oil.
4. Return the air fryer basket to the air fryer and cook for 16 minutes at 200 C (390 F). Serve warm. Enjoy!

Lime Glazed Tofu

Prep Time: 10 Minutes | **Cooking Time:** 14 Minutes | **Servings:** 4 | **Calories:** 284 | **Fat:** 7.9 g | **Carbs:** 38.1 g | **Protein:** 14.8 g

Ingredients and Quantity

- 180 ml coconut aminos
- 2 (400 g) packages extra-firm, water-packed tofu, drained
- 6 tbsp. toasted sesame oil
- 180 ml lime juice

Direction

1. Preheat the air fryer to 200 C (390 F).
2. Pat dry the tofu bars and slice into half-inch cubes.
3. Toss all the ingredients in a small bowl.
4. Marinate for 4 hour in the refrigerator. Drain off the excess water.
5. Place the seasoned tofu cubes in the air fryer basket.
6. Return the air fryer basket to the air fryer and cook for 14 minutes at 200 C (390 F).
7. Toss the tofu once cooked halfway, then resume cooking. Serve warm. Enjoy!

Quinoa Patties

Prep Time: 15 Minutes | **Cooking Time:** 33 Minutes | **Servings:** 4 | **Calories:** 231 | **Fat:** 9 g | **Carbs:** 32.8 g | **Protein:** 6.3 g

Ingredients and Quantity

- 185 g quinoa, red
- 354 ml water
- 1 tsp. salt
- Black pepper, ground
- 120 g rolled oats
- ¾ cup flax egg
- 2 tbsp. minced white onion
- 2 tbsp. crumbled feta cheese
- 2 tbsp. chopped fresh chives
- Salt and black pepper, to taste
- Vegetable or canola oil
- 4 hamburger buns
- 4 rockets
- 4 tomatoes, sliced

For the Cucumber Yogurt Dill Sauce:

- 119 g cucumber, diced
- 245 g Greek yogurt
- 2 tsp. lemon juice
- ¼ tsp. salt
- Ground black pepper, to taste
- 1 tbsp. chopped fresh dill
- 1 tbsp. olive oil

Direction

1. Preheat the Air Fryer to 200 C (390 F).
2. Add quinoa to a saucepan filled with cold water, salt, and black pepper, and place it over medium-high heat.
3. Cook the quinoa to a boil, then reduce the heat, cover, and cook for 20 minutes at 200 C (390 F) on a simmer.
4. Fluff and mix the cooked quinoa with a fork and remove it from the heat.
5. Spread the quinoa in a baking stay.
6. Mix eggs, oats, onion, herbs, cheese, salt, and black pepper.
7. Stir in quinoa, then mix well. Make 4 patties out of this quinoa cheese mixture.
8. Place the patties in the Air Fryer Basket and spray them with cooking oil.
9. Return the Air Fryer Basket to the Air Fryer and cook for 13 minutes.
10. Flip the patties once cooked halfway through, and resume cooking.
11. Meanwhile, prepare the cucumber yoghurt dill sauce by mixing all of its ingredients in a mixing bowl.
12. Place each quinoa patty in a burger bun along with rocket leaves.
13. Serve with yoghurt dill sauce. Enjoy!

Courgette Cakes

Prep Time: 15 Minutes | **Cooking Time:** 17 Minutes | **Servings:** 4 | **Calories:** 270 | **Fat:** 14.6 g | **Carbs:** 31.3 g | **Protein:** 6.4 g

Ingredients and Quantity

- 2 medium courgettes
- 164 g corn kernel
- 1 medium potato, cooked
- 2 tbsp. chickpea flour
- 2 garlic cloves, minced
- 2 tsp. olive oil
- Salt and black pepper, to taste
- Yogurt tahini sauce, for serving

Direction

1. Preheat the air fryer to 200 C (390 F).

2. Mix grated Courgette with a pinch of salt in a colander and leave them for 15 minutes.
3. Squeeze out their excess water.
4. Mash the cooked potato in a large-sized bowl with a fork.
5. Add Courgette, corn, garlic, chickpea flour, salt, and black pepper to the bowl.
6. Mix these fritters' ingredients together and make 2 tablespoons-sized balls out of this mixture and flatten them lightly.
7. Place the fritters in the Air Fryer Basket in a single layer and spray them with cooking.
8. Return the Air Fryer Basket to the Air Fryer and cook for 17 minutes at 200 C (390 F).
9. Flip the fritters once cooked halfway through, then resume cooking. Serve and enjoy!

Cornmeal Hush Puppies

Prep Time: 10 Minutes | **Cooking Time:** 9 Minutes | **Servings:** 6 | **Calories:** 350 | **Fat:** 9.8 g | **Carbs:** 59.6 g | **Protein:** 8.2 g

Ingredients and Quantity

- 210 g fine yellow cornmeal
- 1 tbsp. coconut sugar
- 1 ½ tsp. baking powder
- ½ tsp. garlic powder
- ¼ tsp. salt
- 2 tbsp. jalapeno pepper, chopped
- 15 g yellow onion, chopped
- 120 g almond
- 1 tbsp. almond butter, melted
- 1 tbsp. flaxseed
- 1 tbsp. water
- Non-stick cooking spray

Direction

1. Soak the flaxseeds in a bowl with 1 tablespoon of water for 5 minutes.
2. Mix cornmeal with salt, cayenne pepper, garlic powder, baking powder and coconut sugar in a bowl.
3. Stir in onion and jalapeno, then mix well.
4. Add almond milk, flaxseed mixture and melted butter, then mix until lump-free.
5. Cover and refrigerate for 30 minutes in the refrigerator.
6. Preheat the air fryer to 200 C (390 F).
7. Layer the base of the air fryer basket with a foil sheet and grease with cooking spray.
8. Drop 4 scoops of batter into the air fryer basket.
9. Spray the hush puppies with cooking spray.
10. Air fry them for 9 minutes at 200 C (390 F) in the preheated air fryer.
11. Make more hush puppies with the remaining batter. Serve and enjoy!

Potato Pancakes

Prep Time: 10 Minutes | **Cooking Time:** 10 Minutes | **Servings:** 6 | **Calories:** 134 | **Fat:** 1.9 g | **Carbs:** 26.3 g | **Protein:** 3.8 g

Ingredients and Quantity

- 290 g mashed potatoes
- 3 green onions, sliced
- 1 tsp. oregano
- 1 tsp. smoked paprika
- 2 tbsp. almond flour

Direction

1. Mix the mashed potatoes with green onion, oregano, paprika and flour in a bowl.
2. Make 4 potato patties out of this mixture with wet hands.
3. Preheat the air fryer to 190 C (375 F).

4. Place the paties carefully in the air fryer.
5. Air fry them for 10 minutes at 190 C (375 F), flipping them when cooked halfway through. Serve warm. Enjoy!

Tofu Sandwich

Prep Time: 10 Minutes | **Cooking Time:** 10 Minutes | **Servings:** 4 | **Calories:** 259 | **Fat:** 12.5 g | **Carbs:** 31.8 g | **Protein:** 8 g

Ingredients and Quantity

- 1 block extra-firm tofu, sliced
- ¼ cup light soy sauce
- 1 tsp. garlic powder
- ½ tsp. turmeric
- Dash paprika

For the Sandwich:

- 4 vegan English muffins
- 4 tbsp. vegan mayonnaise
- 1 avocado, sliced
- 4 slices vegan cheese
- 1 onion, sliced
- 1 tomato, sliced

Direction

1. Mix tofu with paprika, turmeric, garlic powder and soy sauce in a bowl.
2. Cover and marinate for 10 minutes.
3. Preheat the air fryer to 200 C (390 F).
4. Place the tofu slices in the preheated air fryer and air fry for 10 minutes at 200 C (390 F).
5. Place the lower half of the English muffins on the working surface.
6. Spread the vegan mayo on top, then add avocado, vegan cheese, onion, tomatoes and a tofu slice on top of each muffin half.
7. Place the rest of the top halves of the English muffins on top. Serve and enjoy!

Tomato Bruschetta

Prep Time: 10 Minutes | **Cooking Time:** 5 Minutes | **Servings:** 4 | **Calories:** 176 | **Fat:** 5.6 g | **Carbs:** 25.2 g | **Protein:** 5.4 g

Ingredients and Quantity

- 4 tomatoes, diced
- 2 garlic cloves, minced
- 2 tsp. fresh basil, chopped
- 2 tsp. olive oil
- 2 tsp. balsamic vinegar
- Salt and black pepper, to taste
- 1 baguette, cut into ½-inch slices

Direction

1. Preheat the air fryer to 190 C (375 F).
2. Place all the baguette slices in the air fryer basket and air fry them for 5 minutes at 190 C (375 F).
3. Mix the tomatoes with garlic, basil, oil, vinegar, black pepper and salt in a bowl.
4. Divide the tomato relish on top of the baguette slices. Serve and enjoy!

Crispy Avocado Tacos

Prep Time: 15 Minutes | **Cooking Time:** 10 Minutes | **Servings:** 12 | **Calories:** 364 | **Fat:** 13.1 g | **Carbs:** 51.8 g | **Protein:** 13.2 g

Ingredients and Quantity

For the Corn and Beans Salad:

- 1 (425 g) can black beans, drained
- 164 g fresh corn
- 2 tbsp. green onion, chopped
- 1 tsp. garlic powder
- ½ tsp. ground cumin
- ½ tsp. coriander
- ½ tsp. mild chipotle chili powder
- 1 fresh lime, juiced
- 75 g salsa

For the Avocado Fries:

- 2 avocados, peeled and cut into 12 slices
- 220 ml aquafaba
- 120 g panko breadcrumbs
- ½ tsp. salt

For the Sriracha Mayo:

- 172 g vegan mayo
- 2 tbsp. sriracha sauce

For the Tacos:

- 12 small corn tortillas, warmed

Direction

1. Preheat the air fryer to 200 C (390 F).
2. Mix all the bean and corn salad ingredients in a bowl.
3. Mix the panko breadcrumbs with salt on a plate and keep it aside.
4. Dip the avocado in the aquafaba and coat it with the panko mixture.
5. Place the avocado in the air fryer and air fry for 10 minutes at 200 C (390 F).
6. Meanwhile, mix sriracha mayo ingredients in a bowl.
7. Spread the avocado slices and corn bean salad on top of the tortillas.
8. Drizzle sriracha mixture on top and serve. Enjoy!

Aubergine Fries

Prep Time: 10 Minutes | **Cooking Time:** 10 Minutes | **Servings:** 2 | **Calories:** 169 | **Fat:** 7.6 g | **Carbs:** 15 g | **Protein:** 13 g

Ingredients and Quantity

- 2 tbsp. flaxseeds
- 2 tbsp. water
- 45 g vegan Parmesan cheese, grated
- 57 g toasted wheat germ
- 1 tsp. Italian seasoning
- 1 medium aubergine
- Non-stick cooking spray

Direction

1. Soak the flaxseeds in water for 5 minutes.
2. Preheat the air fryer to 190 C (375 F).
3. Mix the parmesan cheese, seasonings, and wheat germ in a bowl.
4. Cut the aubergine into ½-inch thick strips and dip them in the flaxseed mixture, then coat with the cheese mixture.
5. Place the aubergines in the air fryer basket and air fry for 10 minutes at 190 C (375 F).
6. Flip the aubergines once cooked halfway through. Serve and enjoy!

Apple Turnovers

Prep Time: 10 Minutes | **Cooking Time:** 6 Minutes | **Servings:** 8 | **Calories:** 194 | **Fat:** 8.8 g | **Carbs:** 28 g | **Protein:** 3.2 g

Ingredients and Quantity

- 2 sheets puff pastry
- 1 tbsp. brown sugar
- ½ tsp. cinnamon
- 1 tbsp. water
- 236 g apple, peeled and diced
- 1 tbsp. lemon juice

Direction

1. Preheat the air fryer to 200 C (390 F).
2. Mix the diced apple with cinnamon, sugar and lemon juice in a bowl.
3. Roll out the puff pastry on a working surface and cut it into four equal-sized squares.
4. Divide the apple mixture onto the center of each square.
5. Fold the squares to make triangles, then crimp the edges with a fork.
6. Brush the triangles with water and place them in the air fryer basket.
7. Air fry the apple turnovers for 6 minutes at 200 C (390 F) until golden brown. Serve and enjoy!

Dessert and Side Recipes

Air Fried Olives

Prep Time: 10 Minutes | **Cooking Time:** 9 Minutes | **Servings:** 4 | **Calories:** 166 | **Fat:** 3.2 g | **Carbs:** 28.8 g | **Protein:** 5.8 g

Ingredients and Quantity

- 360 g blue cheese stuffed olives, drained
- 60 g all-purpose flour
- 150 g panko breadcrumbs
- ½ tsp. garlic powder
- 1 pinch oregano
- 2/4 cup flax egg

Direction

1. Preheat the air fryer to 190 C (375 F).
2. Mix flour with oregano and garlic powder in a bowl and pour the flax egg in another bowl.
3. Spread panko breadcrumbs in a bowl.
4. Coat all the olives with the flour mixture, dip in the eggs and then coat with the panko breadcrumbs.
5. As you coat the olives, place them in the Air Fryer Basket in a single layer, then spray them with cooking oil.
6. Return the Air Fryer Basket to the Air Fryer and cook for 9 minutes at 190 C (375).
7. Flip the olives once cooked halfway through, then resume cooking. Serve and enjoy!

Sweet Potatoes with Maple Butter

Prep Time: 10 Minutes | **Cooking Time:** 40 Minutes | **Servings:** 4 | **Calories:** 288 | **Fat:** 6.9 g | **Carbs:** 46 g | **Protein:** 9.6 g

Ingredients and Quantity

- 4 sweet potatoes, scrubbed
- 1 tsp. olive oil

For the Maple Butter:

- 4 tbsp. unsalted almond butter
- 1 tbsp. maple syrup
- 2 tbsp. hot sauce
- ¼ tsp. salt

Direction

1. Preheat the air fryer to 200 C (390 F).
2. Rub the sweet potatoes with oil and place two potatoes in the Air Fryer Basket.
3. Return the Air Fryer Basket to the Air Fryer and cook for 40 minutes at 200 C (390 F).
4. Flip the potatoes once cooked halfway through, then resume cooking.
5. Mix butter with hot sauce, maple syrup, and salt in a bowl.
6. When the potatoes are done, cut a slit on top and make a well with a spoon.
7. Pour the maple butter into each potato jacket. Serve and enjoy!

Curly Fries

Prep Time: 10 Minutes | **Cooking Time:** 20 Minutes | **Servings:** 4 | **Calories:** 212 | **Fat:** 11.8 g | **Carbs:** 24.6 g | **Protein:** 7.3 g

Ingredients and Quantity

- 2 spiralized courgettes
- 120 g almond flour
- 2 tbsp. paprika
- 1 tsp. cayenne pepper
- 1 tsp. garlic powder
- 1 tsp. black pepper
- 1 tsp. salt
- 2/4 cups applesauce
- Olive oil or non-stick cooking spray

Direction

1. Preheat the air fryer to 200 C (390 F).
2. Mix flour with paprika, cayenne pepper, garlic powder, black pepper, and salt in a bowl.
3. Pour the applesauce in another bowl and dip the Courgette in the applesauce.
4. Coat the Courgette with the flour mixture and place into the Air Fryer Basket.
5. Spray the Courgette with cooking oil.
6. Return the Air Fryer Basket to the Air Fryer and cook for 20 minutes at 200 C (390 F).
7. Toss the Courgette once cooked halfway through, then resume cooking. Serve warm. Enjoy!

Kale Sprouts Salad

Prep Time: 15 Minutes | **Cooking Time:** 8 Minutes | **Servings:** 6 | **Calories:** 221 | **Fat:** 14.6 g | **Carbs:** 15 g | **Protein:** 12.1 g

Ingredients and Quantity

- 1 bunch curly green kale
- 12 Brussels sprouts
- 2 tbsp. sliced almonds
- 20 g shaved vegan Parmesan
- Salt, to taste

For the Tahini-Maple Dressing:

- 4 tbsp. tahini
- 2 tbsp. white wine vinegar
- 2 tsp. white miso
- 2 tsp. choc zero maple syrup
- Pinch red pepper flakes
- 59 ml water

Direction

1. Preheat the air fryer to 200 C (390 F).
2. Toss the Brussels sprouts with salt in a bowl.
3. Spread the Brussels sprouts in the air fryer basket.
4. Air fry them for 8 minutes at 200 C (390 F) and shake once cooked halfway through.
5. Meanwhile, toss all the salad ingredients in a suitable salad bowl.
6. Mix well and stir in the Brussels sprouts. Serve fresh. Enjoy!

Broccoli Salad

Prep Time: 10 Minutes | **Cooking Time:** 6 Minutes | **Servings:** 4 | **Calories:** 203 | **Fat:** 10.3 g | **Carbs:** 25.9 g | **Protein:** 7.6 g

Ingredients and Quantity

- 2 heads broccoli, cut into florets
- 2 tsp. olive oil
- ½ tsp. salt
- 72 g almonds
- 32 g dried cranberries
- 1 tbsp. fresh dill, chopped
- 4 very thin slices lemon

For the Lemony Dressing:

- 96 ml lemon juice
- 1 tbsp. maple syrup
- 1 tsp. Dijon mustard
- 1 tsp. balsamic vinegar

- 1 garlic clove, grated
- 2 tbsp. olive oil

Direction

1. Preheat the air fryer to 180 C (350 F).
2. Toss the broccoli florets with oil and salt in the air fryer basket.
3. Air fry them for 6 minutes at 180 C (350 F) in the air fryer basket.
4. Mix lemon juice, maple syrup, Dijon mustard, vinegar, garlic and olive oil in a salad bowl.
5. Toss in the broccoli, almond, dill, cranberries and lemon slices. Mix well and serve. Enjoy!

Tempeh Caprese Salad

Prep Time: 10 Minutes | **Cooking Time:** 10 Minutes | **Servings:** 4 | **Calories:** 303 | **Fat:** 23.9 g | **Carbs:** 18.6 g | **Protein:** 12.6 g

Ingredients and Quantity

- 1 (16 oz.) block tempeh, diced
- Salt, to taste
- 1 tbsp. olive oil
- Black pepper, to taste

For the Salad:

- 4 ripe tomatoes, cubed
- 113 g vegan Mozzarella cheese, cubed
- 2 avocados, peeled, pitted and cubed
- 3 tbsp. balsamic vinegar
- 3 tbsp. red wine vinegar
- ½ tsp. dried basil
- Salt and ground black pepper, to taste

Direction

1. Preheat your air fryer to 190 C (375 F).
2. Toss the tempeh with black pepper, salt and oil in a bowl.
3. Spread the tempeh cubes in the air fryer basket.
4. Air fry them for 10 minutes at 190 C (375 F) and shake once cooked halfway through.
5. Meanwhile, toss all the salad ingredients in a suitable salad bowl.
6. Mix well and top the salad with tempeh cubes. Serve fresh. Enjoy!

Artichoke Hearts with Garlic Aioli

Prep Time: 10 Minutes | **Cooking Time:** 8 Minutes | **Servings:** 4 | **Calories:** 343 | **Fat:** 14.5 g | **Carbs:** 49 g | **Protein:** 14.5 g

Ingredients and Quantity

For the Artichoke Hearts:

- 14 water-packed artichoke hearts
- 60 g almond flour
- ¼ tsp. baking powder
- 1 pinch salt
- 8 tbsp. water
- 6 tbsp. almond meal
- ¼ tsp. dried basil
- ¼ tsp. dried oregano
- ¼ tsp. paprika
- ¼ tsp. granulated garlic
- Spritz canola oil

For the Lemon Garlic Aioli:

- 200 g vegan mayonnaise
- 1 garlic clove, minced
- 1 tsp. lemon juice
- 1/8 tsp. granulated onion
- Pinch salt

Direction

1. Drain the artichoke and toss with the rest of the ingredients in a bowl.
2. Spread the artichokes in the air fryer basket.
3. Return the basket to the air fryer.
4. Air fry them for 8 minutes at 180 C (350 F) and flip once cooked halfway through.
5. Mix all the garlic aioli ingredients in a bowl. Serve the artichokes with garlic aioli. Enjoy!

Mushroom Skewers

Prep Time: 10 Minutes | **Cooking Time:** 9 Minutes | **Servings:** 6 | **Calories:** 290 | **Fat:** 11.6 g | **Carbs:** 28.5 g | **Protein:** 18.7 g

Ingredients and Quantity

- 4 tbsp. unsalted almond butter
- 3 garlic cloves, minced
- 1 ½ tbsp. soy sauce
- 36 cremini mushrooms with 2-inch caps
- 2 tsp. fresh thyme leaves, chopped
- Salt, to taste

Direction

1. Toss the mushrooms with soy sauce, butter, garlic, thyme and salt in a bowl.
2. Thread these mushrooms on the wooden skewers.
3. Place the seasoned mushrooms in the air fryer basket.
4. Return the basket to the air fryer.
5. Air fry them for 9 minutes at 180 C (350 F) and flip once cooked halfway through. Serve warm. Enjoy!

Sumac Roasted Cauliflower

Prep Time: 10 Minutes | **Cooking Time:** 13 Minutes | **Servings:** 4 | **Calories:** 62 | **Fat:** 2.4 g | **Carbs:** 8.1 g | **Protein:** 2 g

Ingredients and Quantity

- 400 g medium-sized cauliflower florets
- 1 tsp. canola oil
- Pinch salt
- 2 tsp. lemon juice
- 1/8 tsp. sumac

Direction

1. Preheat the air fryer to 200 C (390 F).
2. Toss the cauliflower with lemon and the rest of the ingredients in a bowl.
3. Spread the cauliflower in the air fryer basket.
4. Return the air fryer basket to the air fryer.
5. Air fry the cauliflower for 13 minutes at 200 C (390 F).
6. Shake them once cooked halfway through. Serve and enjoy!

Air Fried Tomatoes

Prep Time: 10 Minutes | **Cooking Time:** 10 Minutes | **Servings:** 4 | **Calories:** 267 | **Fat:** 21.9 g | **Carbs:** 15.5 g | **Protein:** 6.1 g

Ingredients and Quantity

- 60 g almond meal
- 3 tbsp. xanthan gum
- 55 g vegan mayonnaise
- ½ tsp. dried basil
- ½ tsp. dried oregano
- ½ tsp. granulated onion
- Salt and black pepper, to taste
- 1 medium-sized tomatoe, sliced
- Spritz oil spray

Direction

1. Mix mayonnaise, basil, oregano, onion, black pepper, salt, and xanthan gum in a bowl.
2. Dip the tomatoes slices in the mayo mixture.
3. Coat them with almond meal.
4. Place these slices in the Air Fryer basket.
5. Return the basket to the Air Fryer.
6. Air fry them for 10 minutes at 180 C (350 F) and flip once cooked halfway through. Serve warm. Enjoy!

Mushroom Capsicum Kabobs

Prep Time: 10 Minutes | **Cooking Time:** 10 Minutes | **Servings:** 4 | **Calories:** 164 | **Fat:** 13.1 g | **Carbs:** 12.2 g | **Protein:** 3 g

Ingredients and Quantity

- 1 pint whole mushrooms, Portabella
- 1 green capsicum, deseeded and diced
- 1 yellow capsicum, deseeded and diced
- 1 onion, cut into 2-inch pieces
- 1 pint grape tomatoes

For the Marinade:

- 96 ml olive oil
- 2 garlic cloves, minced
- Juice of 1 lemon
- ½ tsp. dried oregano
- ½ tsp. salt

Direction

1. Preheat the air fryer to 200 C (390 F).
2. Toss mushrooms with capsicum and the rest of the ingredients in a bowl.
3. Thread these mushrooms and veggies on the wooden skewers.
4. Place the vegetable skewers in the Air Fryer basket.
5. Return the basket to the Air Fryer.
6. Air fry them for 10 minutes at 200 C (390 F) and flip once cooked halfway through. Serve warm. Enjoy!

Buffalo Cauliflower Steaks

Prep Time: 10 Minutes | **Cooking Time:** 10 Minutes | **Servings:** 2 | **Calories:** 230 | **Fat:** 5.4 g | **Carbs:** 39.6 g | **Protein:** 15 g

Ingredients and Quantity

- 1 large cauliflower head, cut into steaks
- Salt and black pepper, to taste

Dry Ingredients:

- 180 g almond flour
- 50 g xanthan gum
- 1 tbsp. garlic powder
- 1 tbsp. onion powder
- 1 tbsp. salt
- 1 tbsp. paprika
- 2 tsp. cayenne

Wet Ingredients:

- 236 ml soy milk
- 2 tsp. apple cider vinegar
- 2 tbsp. vegan egg powder
- 118 ml ice-cold water
- 2 tbsp. bourbon
- 1 tbsp. hot sauce

Direction

1. Mix the soy milk with all the wet and dry ingredients in a bowl.
2. Dip the cauliflower in the flour batter.
3. Preheat the air fryer to 200 C (390 F).
4. Spread the cauliflower in the air fryer basket.
5. Return the air fryer basket to the air fryer.
6. Air fry the cauliflower for 10 minutes at 200 C (390 F).
7. Shake them once cooked halfway through. Serve and enjoy!

Roasted Buffalo Cauliflower

Prep Time: 15 Minutes | **Cooking Time:** 12 Minutes | **Servings:** 2 | **Calories:** 207 | **Fat:** 14 g | **Carbs:** 17.7 g | **Protein:** 7 g

Ingredients and Quantity

- 213 g broccoli florets
- 192 g cauliflower florets
- 2 tbsp. olive oil
- ½ tsp. garlic powder
- ¼ tsp. salt
- ¼ tsp. paprika
- 1/8 tsp. ground black pepper

Direction

1. Preheat the Air Fryer to 200 C (390 F).
2. Toss cauliflower with broccoli and the rest of the ingredients in a bowl.
3. Spread the cauliflower mixture in the Air Fryer basket.
4. Return the Air Fryer basket to the Air Fryer.
5. Air fry the cauliflower for 12 minutes at 200 C (390 F).
6. Shake them once cooked halfway through. Serve and enjoy!

LOW CARB VEGAN AND VEGETARIAN RECIPES FOR TYPE 2 DIABETES

Appetizer and Snack Recipes

Blistered Shishito Peppers

Prep Time: 10 Minutes | **Cooking Time:** 5 Minutes | **Servings:** 3 | **Calories:** 19 | **Carbs:** 3.8 g | **Protein:** 1.3 g | **Fat:** 0 g | **Sugar:** 2 g | **Sodium:** 4 mg | **Fibre:** 2.5 g

Ingredients and Quantity

- 6 oz. (about 18) Shishito peppers
- Vegetable oil spray
- Coarse sea or kosher salt and lemon wedges, for seasoning

Direction

1. Preheat air fryer to 400 F (205 C).
2. Put the peppers in a bowl and lightly coat them with vegetable oil spray. Toss gently, spray again, and toss until the peppers are glistening but not drenched.
3. Pour the peppers into the basket, spread them into as close to one layer as you can, and air-fry for 5 minutes, tossing and arranging the peppers at the 2 and 4 minutes marks, until the peppers are blistered and even blackened in spots.
4. Pour the peppers into a bowl, add salt to taste, and toss gently. Serve the peppers with wedges to squeeze over them. Enjoy!

Green Olive and Mushroom Tapenade

Prep Time: 10 Minutes | **Cooking Time:** 10 Minutes | **Servings:** 4 | **Calories:** 179 | **Carbs:** 7.5 g | **Protein:** 3.4 g | **Fat:** 17 g | **Sugar:** 1.5 g | **Sodium:** 500 mg | **Fibre:** 3.4 g

Ingredients and Quantity

- ¾ pound brown or Baby Bella mushrooms, sliced
- 1 ½ cups (about ½ pound) pitted green olives
- 3 tbsp. olive oil
- 1 ½ tbsp. fresh oregano leaves, loosely packed
- ¼ tsp. ground black pepper

Direction

1. Preheat the air fryer to 400 F (205 C).
2. When the machine is at temperature, arrange the mushroom slices in as close to an even layer as possible in the basket. They will overlap and even stack on top of each other.
3. Air-fry for 10 minutes, tossing the basket and rearranging the mushrooms every 2 minutes, until shriveled but with still-noticeable moisture.
4. Pour the mushrooms into a food processor. Add the olives, olive oil, oregano leaves, and pepper. Cover and process until grainy, not too much, just not fully smooth for better texture, stopping the machine at least once to scrape down the inside of the canister.
5. Scrape the tapenade into a bowl and serve warm, or cover and refrigerate for up to 4 days. (The

tapenade will taste better if it comes back to room temperature before serving). Enjoy!

Roasted Red Pepper Dip

Prep Time: 10 Minutes | **Cooking Time:** 15 Minutes | **Servings:** 4 | **Calories:** 218 | **Carbs:** 19.6 g | **Protein:** 2.2 g | **Fat:** 11.3 g | **Sugar:** 1.9 g | **Sodium:** 482 mg | **Fibre:** 8 g

Ingredients and Quantity

- 2 medium-red bell peppers
- 1 ¾ cups (one 15 oz. can) canned white beans, drained and rinsed
- 1 tbsp. fresh oregano leaves, packed
- 3 tbsp. olive oil
- 1 tbsp. lemon juice
- ½ tsp. table salt
- ½ tsp. ground black pepper

Direction

1. Preheat the air fryer to 400 F (205 C).
2. Set the peppers in the basket and air-fry undisturbed for 15 minutes, until blistered and even blackened.
3. Use kitchen tongs to transfer the peppers to a zip-closed plastic bag or small bowl. Seal the bag or cover the bowl with plastic wrap. Set aside for 20 minutes.
4. Peel each pepper, then stem it, cut it in half, and remove all its seeds and their white membranes.
5. Set the pieces of the pepper in a food processor. Add the beans, oregano, olive oil, lemon juice, salt, and pepper. Cover and process until smooth, stopping the machine at least once to scrape down the inside of the canister.
6. Scrape the dip into a bowl and serve warm, or cover and refrigerate for up to 3 days (although the dip tastes best if it's allowed to come back to room temperature). Enjoy!

Carrot Chips

Prep Time: 10 Minutes | **Cooking Time:** 10 Minutes | **Servings:** 4 | **Calories:** 107 | **Carbs:** 11 g | **Protein:** 2.2 g | **Fat:** 7 g | **Sugar:** 5 g | **Sodium:** 369 mg | **Fibre:** 2.4 g

Ingredients and Quantity

- 1 pound carrots, thinly sliced
- 2 tbsp. extra-virgin olive oil
- ¼ tsp. garlic powder
- ¼ tsp. black pepper
- ½ tsp. salt

Direction

1. Preheat the air fryer to 390 F (200 C).
2. In a medium bowl, toss the carrot slices with the olive oil, garlic powder, pepper, and salt. Liberally spray the air fryer basket with olive oil mist.
3. Place the carrot slices in the air fryer basket. To allow for even cooking, don't overlap the carrots; cook in batches if necessary.
4. Cook for 5 minutes, shake the basket, and cook another 5 minutes.
5. Remove from the basket and serve warm.
6. Repeat with the remaining carrot slices until they're all cooked. Serve and enjoy!

Okra Chips

Prep Time: 10 Minutes | **Cooking Time:** 16 Minutes | **Servings:** 4 | **Calories:** 103 | **Carbs:** 10.3 g | **Protein:** 2.7 g | **Fat:** 5.5 g | **Sugar:** 2 g | **Sodium:** 448 mg | **Fibre:** 4 g

Ingredients and Quantity

- 1 ¼ pounds thin okra pods, cut into 1-inch pieces
- 1 ½ tbsp. vegetable or canola oil
- ¾ tsp. coarse sea salt or kosher salt

Direction

1. Preheat the air fryer to 400 F (205 C).
2. Toss the okra, oil and salt in a large bowl until the pieces are well and evenly coated
3. When the machine is at temperature, pour the contents of the bowl into the basket.
4. Air-fry, tossing several times, for 16 minutes, or until crisp and quite brown (maybe even a little blackened on the thin bits).
5. Pour the contents of the basket onto a wire rack. Cool for a couple of minutes before serving. Enjoy!

Crispy Spiced Chickpeas

Prep Time: 10 Minutes | **Cooking Time:** 20 Minutes | **Servings:** 4 | **Calories:** 158 | **Carbs:** 19.6 g | **Protein:** 5.3 g | **Fat:** 4.8 g | **Sugar:** 0 g | **Sodium:** 612 mg | **Fibre:** 3.8 g

Ingredients and Quantity

- 1 (15 oz.) can chickpeas, drained (or 1 ½ cups cooked chickpeas)
- ½ tsp. salt
- ½ tsp. chili powder
- ¼ tsp. ground cinnamon
- 1/8 tsp. smoked paprika
- Pinch ground cayenne pepper
- 1 tbsp. olive oil

Direction

1. Preheat the air fryer to 400 F (205 C).
2. Dry the chickpeas as well as you can with a clean kitchen towel, rubbing off any loose skins as necessary. Combine the spices in a small bowl. Toss the chickpeas with the olive oil and then add the spices and toss again.
3. Air-fry for 15 minutes, shaking the basket a couple of times while they cook.
4. Check the chickpeas to see if they are crispy enough and if necessary, air-fry for another 5 minutes to crisp them further.
5. Serve warm, or cool to room temperature and store in an airtight container for up to two weeks. Enjoy!

Halloumi Fries

Prep Time: 10 Minutes | **Cooking Time:** 12 Minutes | **Servings:** 4 | **Calories:** 355 | **Carbs:** 2.2 g | **Protein:** 18.4 g | **Fat:** 30.4 g | **Sugar:** 2 g | **Sodium:** 438 mg | **Fibre:** 0 g

Ingredients and Quantity

- 1 ½ tbsp. olive oil
- 1 ½ tsp. minced garlic
- 1/8 tsp. dried oregano
- 1/8 tsp. dried thyme
- 1/8 tsp. table salt
- 1/8 tsp. ground black pepper

- ¾ pound halloumi

Direction

1. Preheat the air fryer to 400 F (205 C).
2. Whisk the oil, garlic, oregano, thyme, salt and pepper in a medium bowl.
3. Lay the piece of halloumi flat on a cutting board. Slice it widthwise into ½ inch thick sticks. Then cut each stick lengthwise into ½-inch thick batons.
4. Put these batons into the olive oil mixture. Toss gently, until well coated.
5. Place the batons in the basket in a single layer. Air-fry undisturbed for 12 minutes, or until lightly browned, particularly at the edges.
6. Transfer the fried into a wire rack. They may need a little coaxing with a nonstick-safe spatula to come free. Cool for a couple of minutes before serving hot. Enjoy!

Cinnamon Apple Crisps

Prep Time: 10 Minutes | **Cooking Time:** 22 Minutes | **Servings:** 2 | **Calories:** 66 | **Carbs:** 16 g | **Protein:** 0.4 g | **Fat:** 0.8 g | **Sugar:** 7 g | **Sodium:** 1 mg | **Fibre:** 3.2 g

Ingredients and Quantity

- 1 large apple
- ½ tsp. ground cinnamon
- 2 tsp. avocado oil or coconut oil

Direction

1. Preheat the air fryer to 300 F (150 C).
2. Using a mandolin or knife, slice the apples to 1/4-inch thickness. Pat the apples dry with a paper towel or kitchen cloth.
3. Sprinkle the apple slices with ground cinnamon. Spray or drizzle the oil over the top of the apple slices and toss to coat.
4. Place the apple slices in the air fryer. To allow for even cooking, do not overlap the slices. Cook in batches if necessary.
5. Cook for 20 minutes, shaking the basket every 5 minutes. After 20 minutes, increase the air fryer temperature to 330 F and cook for another 2 minutes, shaking every 30 seconds. Remove the apples from the basket immediately, before they get too dark.
6. Spread the chips out onto paper towels to cool completely, for at least 5 minutes.
7. Repeat the above steps for the remaining apple slices until they are all cooked. Serve and enjoy!

Crispy Tofu Bites

Prep Time: 10 Minutes | **Cooking Time:** 20 Minutes | **Servings:** 4 | **Calories:** 79 | **Carbs:** 1.9 g | **Protein:** 9.3 g | **Fat:** 4.7 g | **Sugar:** 0.7 g | **Sodium:** 14 mg | **Fibre:** 1 g

Ingredients and Quantity

- 1 pound extra firm unflavoured tofu
- Vegetable oil spray

Direction

1. Wrap the piece of tofu in a triple layer of paper towels. Place it on a wooden cutting board and set a large pot on top of it to press out excess moisture. Set aside for 10 minutes.
2. Preheat the air fryer to 400 F (205 C).

3. Remove the pot and unwrap the tofu. Cut it into 1-inch cubes.
4. Place these in a bowl and coat them generously with vegetable oil spray. Toss gently, then spray generously again before tossing, until all are glistening.
5. Gently pour the tofu pieces into the basket, spread them into as close to one layer as possible, and air-fry for 20 minutes, using kitchen tongs to gently rearrange the pieces at the 7 and 14-minute marks, until light brown and crisp.
6. Gently pour the tofu pieces onto a wire rack. Cool for 5 minutes before serving warm. Enjoy!

Zucchini Chips

Prep Time: 10 Minutes | **Cooking Time:** 17 Minutes | **Servings:** 3 | **Calories:** 33 | **Carbs:** 6.9 g | **Protein:** 2.5 g | **Fat:** 0.4 g | **Sugar:** 3.6 g | **Sodium:** 215 mg | **Fibre:** 2.3 g

Ingredients and Quantity

- 1 ½ small (about 1 ½ cups) zucchini, washed but not peeled, and cut into ¼-inch thick rounds
- Olive oil spray
- ¼ tsp. table salt

Direction

1. Preheat the air fryer to 375 F (190 C).
2. Lay some paper towels on your work surface. Set the zucchini rounds on top, then set more paper towels over the rounds. Press gently to remove some of the moisture.
3. Remove the top layer of paper towels and lightly coat the rounds with olive oil spray on both sides.
4. When the machines is at temperature, set the rounds in the basket, overlapping them a bit as needed. They will shrink as they cook. Aif-fry for 15 minutes, tossing and rearranging the rounds at the 5 and 10-minute mark, until browned, soft, yet crisp at the edges.
5. **NOTE:** You will need to air-fry the rounds 2 minutes more if the temperature is set 360 F (182 C).
6. Gently pour the contents of the basket onto a wire rack. Cool for at least 10 minutes or up to 2 hours before serving. Enjoy!

Za'atar Garbanzo Beans

Prep Time: 10 Minutes | **Cooking Time:** 12 Minutes | **Servings:** 6 | **Calories:** 102 | **Carbs:** 15.6 g | **Protein:** 3.4 g | **Fat:** 3.1 g | **Sugar:** 0 g | **Sodium:** 233 mg | **Fibre:** 3.1 g

Ingredients and Quantity

- 1 (14.5 oz.) can garbanzo beans, drained and rinsed
- 1 tbsp. extra-virgin olive oil
- 6 tsp. za'atar seasoning mix
- 2 tbsp. chopped parsley
- Salt and pepper, to taste

Direction

1. Preheat the air fryer to 390 F (200 C).
2. In a medium bowl, toss the garbanzo beans with olive oil and za'atar seasoning.
3. Pour the beans into the air fryer basket and cook for 12 minutes, or until toasted as you like. Stir every 3 minutes while roasting.
4. Remove the beans from the air fryer basket into a serving bowl, top with fresh chopped parsley, and season with salt and pepper. Enjoy!

Potato Appetizer with Garlic-Mayo Sauce

Servings: 4 | **Total Time:** 20 Minutes | **Calories:** 277 | **Fat:** 50 g | **Protein:** 1.7 g | **Carbs:** 6 g | **Fiber:** 3 g

Ingredients and Quantity

- 2 tbsp. vegetable oil of your choice
- Kosher salt and freshly ground black pepper, to taste
- 3 Russet potatoes, cut into wedges

For the Dipping Sauce:

- 2 tsp. dried rosemary, crushed
- 3 garlic cloves, minced
- 1/3 tsp. dried marjoram, crushed
- ¼ cup full-fat coconut milk
- 1/3 cup vegan mayonnaise

Direction

1. Lightly grease your potatoes with a thin layer of vegetable oil.
2. Season with salt and ground black pepper.
3. Arrange the seasoned potato wedges in an air fryer cooking basket.
4. Bake at 395 degrees F (200 C) for 15 minutes, shaking once or twice.
5. In the meantime, prepare the dipping sauce by mixing all the sauce ingredients.
6. Serve the potatoes with the dipping sauce and enjoy!

Breakfast Recipes

Shoestring Butternut Squash Fries

Prep Time: 10 Minutes | **Cooking Time:** 16 Minutes | **Servings:** 3 | **Calories:** 68 | **Carbs:** 15.6 g | **Protein:** 2.2 g | **Fat:** 0.2 g | **Sugar:** 3.3 g | **Sodium:** 56 mg | **Fibre:** 3 g

Ingredients and Quantity

- 1 pound 2 oz. spiralized butternut squash strands
- Vegetable oil spray
- Coarse sea salt and kosher salt, to taste

Direction

1. Preheat the air fryer to 375 F (190 C).
2. Place the spiralized squash in a big bowl. Coat the strands with vegetable oil spray, toss well, coat again, and toss several times to make sure all the strands have been oiled.
3. When the machine is at temperature, pour the strands into the basket and spread them out into as even a layer as possible.
4. Air-fry for 16 minutes, tossing and rearranging the strands every 4 minutes, or until they're lightly browned and crisp.
5. Pour the contents of the basket into a serving bowl, add salt to taste, and toss well before serving hot. Enjoy!

Charred Radicchio Salad

Prep Time: 10 Minutes | **Cooking Time:** 5 Minutes | **Servings:** 4 | **Calories:** 108 | **Carbs:** 3.3 g | **Protein:** 1 g | **Fat:** 10.7 g | **Sugar:** 0.5 g | **Sodium:** 307 mg | **Fibre:** 0.7 g

Ingredients and Quantity

- 2 (5 to 6 oz.) radicchio heads
- 3 tbsp. olive oil
- ½ tsp. table salt
- 2 tbsp. Balsamic vinegar
- ¼ tsp. red pepper flakes

Direction

1. Preheat the air fryer to 375 F (190 C).
2. Cut the radicchio heads into quarters through the stem end. Brush the oil over the heads, particularly getting it between the leaves along the cut sides.
3. Sprinkle the radicchio quarters with the salt.
4. When the machine is at temperature, set the quarters cut sides up in the basket with as much air space between them as possible. They should not touch.
5. Air-fry undisturbed for 5 minutes, watching carefully because they burn quickly, until blackened in bits and soft.
6. Use a nonstick-safe spatula to transfer the quarters to a cutting board.
7. Cool for a minute or two, then cut out the thick stems inside the heads.
8. Discard these tough bits and chop the remaining heads into bite-size bits.
9. Scrape them into a bowl. Add the vinegar and red pepper flakes. Toss well and serve warm. Enjoy!

Roasted Peppers with Balsamic Vinegar and Basil

Prep Time: 10 Minutes | **Cooking Time:** 12 Minutes | **Servings:** 6 | **Calories:** 86 | **Carbs:** 6 g | **Protein:** 0.8 g | **Fat:** 13.1 g | **Sugar:** 4 g | **Sodium:** 4 mg | **Fibre:** 1.1 g

Ingredients and Quantity

- 4 small or medium red or yellow bell peppers
- 3 tbsp. olive oil
- 1 tbsp. Balsamic vinegar
- 6 fresh basil leaves, torn up

Direction

1. Preheat the air fryer to 400 F (205 C).
2. When the machine is at temperature, put the peppers in the basket with at least ¼ inch between them.
3. Air-fry undisturbed for 12 minutes, until blistered, even blackened in places.
4. Use kitchen tongs to transfer the peppers to a medium bowl. Cover the bowl with plastic wrap. Set aside at room temperature for 30 minutes.
5. Uncover the bowl and use kitchen tongs to transfer the peppers to a cutting board or work surface.
6. Peel off the filmy exterior skin. If there are blackened bits under it, these can stay on the peppers.
7. Cut off and remove the stem ends. Split open the peppers and discard any seeds and their spongy membranes.
8. Slice the peppers into ½-inch- to 1-inch-wide strips.
9. Put these in a clean bowl and gently toss them with the oil, vinegar, and basil. Serve at once, or cover and store at room temperature for up to 4 hours or in the refrigerator for up to 5 days. Enjoy!

Sweet Potato Curly Fries

Prep Time: 10 Minutes | **Cooking Time:** 10 Minutes | **Servings:** 4 | **Calories:** 142 | **Carbs:** 19.6 g | **Protein:** 1.9 g | **Fat:** 5.4 g | **Sugar:** 0.6 g | **Sodium:** 447 mg | **Fibre:** 5 g

Ingredients and Quantity

- 2 medium sweet potatoes, washed
- 2 tbsp. avocado oil
- ¾ tsp. salt, divided
- 1 medium avocado
- ½ tsp. garlic powder
- ½ tsp. paprika
- ¼ tsp. black pepper
- ½ juice lime
- 3 tbsp. fresh cilantro

Direction

1. Preheat the air fryer to 400 F (205 C).
2. Using a spiralizer, create curly spirals with the sweet potatoes. Keep the pieces about 1½ inches long. Continue until all the potatoes are used.
3. In a large bowl, toss the curly sweet potatoes with the avocado oil and ½ teaspoon of the salt.
4. Place the potatoes in the air fryer basket and cook for 5 minutes; shake and cook another 5 minutes.
5. While cooking, add the avocado, garlic, paprika, pepper, the remaining ¼ teaspoon of salt, lime juice, and cilantro to a blender and process until smooth. Set aside.
6. When cooking completes, remove the fries and serve warm with the lime avocado sauce. Enjoy!

Roasted Yellow Squash and Onions

Prep Time: 10 Minutes | **Cooking Time:** 20 Minutes | **Servings:** 3 | **Calories:** 36 | **Carbs:** 7.8 g | **Protein:** 1.5 g | **Fat:** 0.3 g | **Sugar:** 3.7 g | **Sodium:** 584 mg | **Fibre:** 2 g

Ingredients and Quantity

- 1 medium (8-inch) yellow or summer crookneck squash, cut into ½-inch thick rounds
- 1 ½ cups (1 large onion) yellow or white onion, roughly chopped
- ¾ tsp. table salt
- ¼ tsp. ground cumin (optional)
- Olive oil spray
- 1 ½ tbsp. lemon or lime juice

Direction

1. Preheat the air fryer to 375 F (190 C).
2. Toss the squash rounds, onion, salt, and cumin (if using) in a large bowl. Lightly coat the vegetables with olive oil spray, toss again, spray again, and keep at it until the vegetables are evenly coated.
3. When the machine is at temperature, scrape the contents of the bowl into the basket, spreading the vegetables out into as close to one layer as you can.
4. Air-fry for 20 minutes, tossing once very gently, until the squash and onions are soft, even a little browned at the edges.
5. Pour the contents of the basket into a serving bowl, add the lemon or lime juice, and toss gently but well to coat. Serve warm or at room temperature. Enjoy!

Blistered Tomatoes

Prep Time: 10 Minutes | **Cooking Time:** 15 Minutes | **Servings:** 20 | **Calories:** 6 | **Carbs:** 1.3 g | **Protein:** 2.2 g | **Fat:** 0.1 g | **Sugar:** 0.9 g | **Sodium:** 33 mg | **Fibre:** 0.4 g

Ingredients and Quantity

- 1 ½ pounds cherry or grape tomatoes
- Olive oil spray
- 1 ½ tsp. Balsamic vinegar
- ¼ tsp. table salt
- ¼ tsp. ground black pepper

Direction

1. Put the basket in a drawer-style air fryer, or a baking tray in the lower third of a toaster oven–style air fryer.
2. Place a 6-inch round cake pan in the basket or on the tray for a small batch, a 7-inch round cake pan for a medium batch, or an 8-inch round cake pan for a large one.
3. Heat the air fryer to 400 F (205 C) with the pan in the basket. When the machine is at temperature, keep heating the pan for 5 minutes more.
4. Place the tomatoes in a large bowl, coat them with the olive oil spray, toss gently, then spritz a couple of times more, tossing after each spritz, until the tomatoes are glistening.
5. Pour the tomatoes into the cake pan and air-fry undisturbed for 10 minutes, or until they split and begin to brown.
6. Use kitchen tongs and a nonstick-safe spatula, or silicone baking mitts, to remove the cake pan from the basket.
7. Toss the hot tomatoes with the vinegar, salt, and pepper. Cool in the pan for a few minutes before serving. Enjoy!

Fried Cauliflower with Parmigiano-Reggiano Lemon Dressing

Prep Time: 10 Minutes | **Cooking Time:** 12 Minutes | **Servings:** 4 | **Calories:** 197 | **Carbs**: 5.5 g | **Protein:** 4.1 g | **Fat:** 19.1 g | **Sugar:** 2.5 g | **Sodium:** 209 mg | **Fibre:** 2.6 g

Ingredients and Quantity

- 4 cups cauliflower florets (about half a large head)
- 1 tbsp. olive oil
- Salt and freshly ground black pepper
- 1 tsp. finely chopped lemon zest
- 1 tbsp. fresh lemon juice (from about half a lemon)
- ¼ cup grated Parmigiano-Reggiano cheese
- 4 5bsp. extra virgin olive oil
- ¼ tsp. salt
- Freshly ground pepper, to taste
- 1 tbsp. chopped fresh parsley

Direction

1. Preheat the air fryer to 400 F (205 C).
2. Toss the cauliflower florets with the olive oil, salt and freshly ground black pepper.
3. Air-fry for 12 minutes, shaking the basket a couple of times during the cooking process.
4. While the cauliflower is frying, make the dressing. Combine the lemon zest, lemon juice, Parmigiano-Reggiano cheese and olive oil in a small bowl.
5. Season with salt and lots of freshly ground black pepper. Stir in the parsley.
6. Transfer the fried cauliflower into a serving platter and drizzle the dressing over the top. Serve and enjoy!

Roman Artichokes

Prep Time: 10 Minutes | **Cooking Time:** 12 Minutes | **Servings:** 4 | **Calories:** 108 | **Carbs:** 14 g | **Protein:** 4.3 g | **Fat:** 5.5 g | **Sugar:** 1.3 g | **Sodium:** 702 mg | **Fibre:** 7 g

Ingredients and Quantity

- 2 (9 oz.) boxes frozen artichoke heart quarters, thawed
- 1 ½ tbsp. olive oil
- 2 tsp. minced garlic
- 1 tsp. table salt
- ½ tsp. red pepper flakes

Direction

1. Preheat the air fryer to 400 F (205 C).
2. Gently toss the artichoke heart quarters, oil, garlic, salt, and red pepper flakes in a bowl until the quarters are well coated.
3. When the machine is at temperature, scrape the contents of the bowl into the basket. Spread the artichoke heart quarters out into as close to one layer as possible.
4. Air-fry undisturbed for 8 minutes. Gently toss and rearrange the quarters so that any covered or touching parts are now exposed to the air currents, then air-fry undisturbed for 4 minutes more, until very crisp.
5. Gently pour the contents of the basket onto a wire rack. Cool for a few minutes before serving. Enjoy!

Eggplant Salad

Servings: 2 | **Total Time:** 35 Minutes | **Calories:** 133 | **Fat:** 12 g | **Protein:** 3 g | **Carbs:** 5 g | **Fiber:** 1.3 g

Ingredients and Quantity

- 2 large eggplants
- 1 tsp. vinegar
- 1 garlic clove
- 4 spring onions
- 1 shallot
- 2 parsley stalks
- Black pepper and salt

Direction

1. Peel and cut the eggplants into large pieces.
2. Cook in the air fryer over high heat with boiling water for about 20 minutes.
3. Lower the heat and cook for another 20 minutes.
4. Let cool and crush with a fork.
5. Drizzle the eggplant with a well-seasoned vinaigrette dressing with chopped garlic, chives, and shallot in very small pieces.
6. Sprinkle the chopped parsley and serve very cold. Enjoy!

Parsley Tomatoes

Servings: 2 | **Total Time:** 28 Minutes | **Calories:** 57 | **Fat:** 0 g | **Protein:** 3 g | **Carbs:** 6 g | **Fiber:** 0.5 g

Ingredients and Quantity

- 4 ripe tomatoes
- 1 red or white onion, cut into 8 equal parts
- 2 minced garlic cloves
- 5 jalapeno peppers
- 1 ½ L lemon juice
- Some coriander stalks
- A pinch salt

Direction

1. Cook tomatoes in the air fryer for 30 seconds.
2. Peel and remove the seeds in the mixer container.
3. Put the onion pieces, the garlic, and the salt.
4. Remove the peduncle from the jalapeno peppers and cut them in two.
5. Save some seeds for a more or less spicy sauce.
6. Cut the peppers roughly and add the desired amount of seeds to the mixer bowl.
7. Grind until the sauce reaches the desired consistency.
8. Transfer the sauce to a pan and cook in the air fryer at medium temperature until it is covered in a pink foam, which should take about 6 to 8 minutes to cook.
9. Remove from heat and let cool for at least 10 minutes.
10. Add lemon juice and coriander. Serve and enjoy!

Eggplants with Garlic and Parsley

Servings: 2 | **Total Time:** 50 Minutes | **Calories:** 110 | **Fat:** 10 g | **Protein:** 1 g | **Carbs:** 3 g | **Fiber:** 1.1 g

Ingredients and Quantity

- 200 to 250 g eggplant
- 1 garlic clove
- 2 parsley stalks
- Black pepper and salt, to taste

Direction

1. Remove the stalks, wash, and dry the eggplants.

2. Cut them in two lengthwise. Remove the pulp from the eggplants.
3. Chop the garlic, parsley and eggplant pulp.
4. Season adequately using salt along with pepper.
5. Fill the eggplants with the mixture.
6. Close them in foil and cook in the air fryer for about 30 to 35 minutes at 170 degrees C. Serve and enjoy!

Perfect Broccoli

Prep Time: 10 Minutes | **Cooking Time:** 12 Minutes | **Servings:** 4 | **Calories:** 39 | **Carbs:** 7.6 g | **Protein:** 3.2 g | **Fat:** 13.1 g | **Sugar:** 1.9 g | **Sodium:** 474 mg | **Fibre:** 3 g

Ingredients and Quantity

- 5 cups (about 1 pound 10 oz.) 1 to 1 ½ inches fresh broccoli florets (not frozen)
- Olive oil spray
- ¾ tsp. table salt

Direction

1. Preheat the air fryer to 375 F (190 C).
2. Put the broccoli florets in a big bowl, coat them generously with olive oil spray, then toss to coat all surfaces, even down into the crannies, spraying them in a couple of times more. Sprinkle the salt on top and toss again.
3. When the machine is at temperature, pour the florets into the basket. Air-fry for 10 minutes, tossing and rearranging the pieces twice so that all the covered or touching bits are eventually exposed to the air currents, until lightly browned but still crunchy.
4. **NOTE:** If the machine is at 360 F (185 C), you may have to add 2 minutes to the cooking time.
5. Pour the florets into a serving bowl. Cool for a minute or two, then serve hot. Enjoy!

Roasted Cauliflower with Garlic and Capers

Prep Time: 10 Minutes | **Cooking Time:** 10 Minutes | **Servings:** 3 | **Calories:** 109 | **Carbs:** 6.2 g | **Protein:** 2.2 g | **Fat:** 9.5 g | **Sugar:** 2.5 g | **Sodium:** 352 mg | **Fibre:** 2.7 g

Ingredients and Quantity

- 3 cups (about 15 oz.) 1-inch cauliflower florets
- 2 tbsp. olive oil
- 1 ½ tbsp. drained and rinsed capers, chopped
- 2 tsp. minced garlic
- ¼ tsp. table salt
- ¼ tsp. red pepper flakes

Direction

1. Preheat the air fryer to 375 F (190 C).
2. Stir the cauliflower florets, olive oil, capers, garlic, salt, and red pepper flakes in a large bowl until the florets are evenly coated.
3. When the machine is at temperature, put the florets in the basket, spreading them out to as close to one layer as you can.
4. Air-fry for 10 minutes, tossing once to get any covered pieces exposed to the air current, until tender and lightly browned.
5. Transfer the contents of the basket into a serving bowl/platter. Cool for a minute or two before serving. Enjoy!

Tandoori Cauliflower

Prep Time: 10 Minutes | **Cooking Time:** 10 Minutes | **Servings:** 4 | **Calories:** 53 | **Carbs:** 8.6 g | **Protein:** 4.1 g | **Fat:** 0.6 g | **Sugar:** 4 g | **Sodium:** 494 mg | **Fibre:** 3.1 g

Ingredients and Quantity

- ½ cup plain full-fat yogurt (not Greek yogurt)
- 1 ½ tsp. yellow curry powder, purchased or homemade
- 1 ½ tsp. lemon juice
- ¾ tsp. table salt (optional)
- 4 ½ cups (about 1 pounds 2 oz.) 2 inches cauliflower florets

Direction

1. Preheat the air fryer to 400 F (205 C).
2. Whisk the yogurt, curry powder, lemon juice, and salt (if using) in a large bowl until uniform. Add the florets and stir gently to coat the florets well and evenly. Even better, use your clean, dry hands to get the yogurt mixture down into all the nooks of the florets.
3. When the machine is at temperature, transfer the florets to the basket, spreading them gently into as close to one layer as you can.
4. Air-fry for 10 minutes, tossing and rearranging the florets twice so that any covered or touching parts are exposed to the air currents, until lightly browned and tender if still a bit crunchy.
5. Pour the contents of the basket onto a wire rack. Cool for at least 5 minutes before serving, or serve at room temperature. Enjoy!

Tomato Candy

Prep Time: 10 Minutes | **Cooking Time:** 120 Minutes | **Servings:** 12 | **Calories:** 8 | **Carbs:** 1.8 g | **Protein:** 0.4 g | **Fat:** 0.1 g | **Sugar:** 1.2 g | **Sodium:** 293 mg | **Fibre:** 0.6 g

Ingredients and Quantity

- 6 small Roma tomatoes, halved lengthwise
- 1 ½ tsp. coarse sea salt or kosher salt

Direction

1. Before you turn the machine on, set the tomatoes cut side up in a single layer in the basket (or the basket attachment). They can touch each other, but try to leave at least a fraction of an inch between them (depending, of course, on the size of the basket or basket attachment). Sprinkle the cut sides of the tomatoes with the salt.
2. Set the machine to cook at 225 F or 107 C (or 230 F, if that's the closest setting).
3. Put the basket in the machine and air-fry for 2 hours, or until the tomatoes are dry but pliable, with a little moisture down in their centers.
4. Remove the basket from the machine and cool the tomatoes in it for 10 minutes before gently transferring them to a plate for serving, or to a shallow dish that you can cover and store in the refrigerator for up to 1 week. Enjoy!

Roasted Garlic and Thyme Tomatoes

Prep Time: 10 Minutes | **Cooking Time:** 15 Minutes | **Servings:** 2 | **Calories:** 107 | **Carbs:** 10.2 g | **Protein:** 2.3 g | **Fat:** 7.5 g | **Sugar:** 4 g | **Sodium:** 90 mg | **Fibre:** 3.1 g

Ingredients and Quantity

- 4 Roma tomatoes
- 1 tbsp. olive oil
- Salt and freshly ground black pepper
- 1 garlic clove, minced
- ½ tsp. dried thyme

Direction

1. Preheat the air fryer to 390 F (200 C).
2. Cut the tomatoes in half and scoop out the seeds and any pithy parts with your fingers.
3. Place the tomatoes in a bowl and toss with the olive oil, salt, pepper, garlic and thyme.
4. Transfer the tomatoes to the air fryer, with the cut side facing up.
5. Air-fry for 15 minutes. The edge should just start to brown.
6. Allow the tomatoes to cool to an edible temperature for a few minutes, and then use in pastas, on top of crostini, or serve with any poultry, meat or fish. Enjoy!

Simple Cauliflower

Prep Time: 10 Minutes | **Cooking Time:** 6 Minutes | **Servings:** 4 | **Calories:** 19 | **Carbs:** 4.1 g | **Protein:** 1.5 g | **Fat:** 0.1 g | **Sugar:** 1.7 g | **Sodium:** 22 mg | **Fibre:** 3.9 g

Ingredients and Quantity

- ½ cup water
- 1 (10 oz.) package frozen cauliflower
- 1 tsp. lemon pepper seasoning

Direction

1. Pour water into the air fryer drawer.
2. Pour the frozen cauliflower into the air fryer basket and sprinkle with lemon pepper seasoning.
3. Cook at 390 F (200 C) for about 6 minutes. Serve and enjoy!

Vegetable Couscous

Prep Time: 10 Minutes | **Cooking Time:** 10 Minutes | **Servings:** 4 | **Calories:** 168 | **Carbs:** 19.6 g | **Protein:** 5.6 g | **Fat:** 3.9 g | **Sugar:** 1.6 g | **Sodium:** 84 mg | **Fibre:** 2 g

Ingredients and Quantity

- 4 oz. white mushrooms, sliced
- ½ medium-size green bell pepper, julienned
- 1 cup cubed zucchini
- ¼ small onion, slivered
- 1 stalk celery, thinly sliced
- ¼ tsp. ground coriander
- ¼ tsp. ground cumin
- Salt and pepper
- 1 tbsp. olive oil
- ¾ cup uncooked couscous
- 1 cup vegetable broth or water
- ½ tsp. salt (Omit if using salted broth)

Direction

1. Combine all vegetables in large bowl. Sprinkle with coriander, cumin, and salt and pepper to taste. Stir well, add olive oil, and stir again to coat vegetables evenly.
2. Place vegetables in air fryer basket and cook at 390 F (200 C) for 5 minutes. Stir and cook for 5 more minutes, until tender.

3. While vegetables are cooking, prepare the couscous: Place broth or water and salt in a large saucepan. Heat to boiling, stir in the conscous, cover and remove from heat.

4. Allow the couscous to sit for 5 minutes, stir in cooked vegetables, and serve hot. Enjoy!

Vegan Breakfast Ranchero

Servings: 2 | **Total Time:** 13 Minutes

Ingredients and Quantity

- 2 large flour gluten-free tortillas
- 2 small corn tortillas
- 2 servings vegan scramble or tofu scramble
- ½ to 1 cup classic jarred Ranchero sauce
- ½ to ¾ avocado, peeled and sliced lengthways
- 1 to 2 fresh jalapenos, stemmed, pitted and sliced
- 1/3 cup cooked pinto beans

Direction

1. Arrange the large flour tortillas onto your work surface.
2. Assemble the wraps by stacking all ingredients in to the tortilla in this order - egg or tofu scramble, the jalapeno, jarred Ranchero sauce, fresh corn tortillas, sliced avocado and finally the cooked pinto beans.
3. You may add additional ranchero sauce as per your preference.
4. Fold the flour tortilla around the fillings until they are completely sealed. It should resemble a traditional burrito.
5. Cook in the air fryer at 350 degrees Fahrenheit (180 C) for 6 minutes and then bake in the oven at 325 degrees Fahrenheit (163 C) for 5-8 minutes, until warm and slightly crispy.
6. Finally, pan fry in dry pan at a medium-low heat for a 2 - 3 minutes on each side, until crisp and golden brown.
7. Serve immediately with traditional Mexican toppings like sour cream, guacamole or Queso fresco. Enjoy!

Lunch Recipes

Air Fried Cheesy Onions

Prep Time: 10 Minutes | **Cooking Time:** 18 Minutes | **Servings:** 4 | **Calories:** 72 | **Carbs:** 14 g | **Protein:** 2.8 g | **Fat:** 4.7 g | **Sugar:** 2.4 g | **Sodium:** 29 mg | **Fibre:** 1.3 g

Ingredients and Quantity

- 2 yellow onions (I recommend Vidalia or 1015)
- Salt and pepper, to taste
- ¼ tsp. ground thyme
- ¼ tsp. smoked paprika
- 2 tsp. olive oil
- 1 oz. vegan Gruyere cheese, grated

Direction

1. Peel onions and halve lengthwise (vertically).
2. Sprinkle cut sides of onions with salt, pepper, thyme, and paprika.
3. Place each onion half, cut-surface up, on a large square of aluminum foil. Pull sides of foil up to cup around onion.
4. Drizzle cut surface of onions with oil. Crimp foil at top to seal closed.
5. Place wrapped onions in air fryer basket and cook at 390 F (200 C) for 18 minutes. When done, onions should be soft enough to pierce with fork but still slightly firm.
6. Open foil just enough to sprinkle each onion with grated cheese.
7. Cook for 30 seconds to 1 minute to melt cheese. Serve and enjoy!

Sauteed Mushrooms

Prep Time: 10 Minutes | **Cooking Time:** 4 Minutes | **Servings:** 4 | **Calories:** 33 | **Carbs:** 5.5 g | **Protein:** 3.6 g | **Fat:** 13.1 g | **Sugar:** 3.5 g | **Sodium:** 89 mg | **Fibre:** 1.2 g

Ingredients and Quantity

- 8 oz. sliced white mushrooms, rinsed and well drained
- ¼ tsp. garlic powder
- 1 tbsp. Worcestershire sauce

Direction

1. Place mushrooms in a large bowl and sprinkle with garlic powder and Worcestershire. Stir well to distribute seasons evenly.
2. Place the air fryer basket and cook at 390 F (200 C) for 4 minutes, until tender. Serve and enjoy!

Tricolor Spinach

Servings: 4 | **Total Time:** 1 Hour 20 Minutes | **Calories:** 68 | **Fat:** 4 g | **Protein:** 3 g | **Carbs:** 4 g | **Fiber:** 0.6 g

Ingredients and Quantity

- 400 g frozen spinach
- 3 tomatoes
- 2 peppers

- Some thyme stems
- 1 bay leaf
- Black pepper and salt, to taste

Direction

1. Thaw spinach as directed in the total time required to prepare mode.
2. In a saucepan, place the sliced tomatoes, sliced peppers, thyme, bay leaf, and a glass of water.
3. Season adequately using salt along with pepper.
4. Cook for 10 minutes over low heat in an air fryer.
5. Add spinach and serve very hot. Enjoy!

Easy Cheesy Broccoli

Servings: 4 | **Total Time:** 25 Minutes | **Calories:** 103 | **Fat:** 9.1 g | **Protein:** 1.9 g | **Carbs:** 4.9 g | **Fiber:** 1.2 g

Ingredients and Quantity

- 1/3 cup grated vegan yellow cheese
- 1 large-sized head broccoli, stemmed and cut small florets
- 2 ½ tbsp. canola oil
- 2 tsp. dried rosemary
- 2 tsp. dried basil
- Salt and ground black pepper, to taste

Direction

1. Bring a medium pan filled with a lightly salted water to a boil.
2. Then, boil the broccoli florets for about 3 minutes.
3. Then, drain the broccoli florets well; toss them with the canola oil, rosemary, basil, salt and black pepper.
4. Set your air fryer to 390 degrees F (200 C); arrange the seasoned broccoli in the cooking basket; set the timer for 17 minutes.
5. Toss the broccoli halfway through the cooking process.
6. Serve warm topped with grated cheese and enjoy!

Stuffed Mushrooms

Servings: 2 | **Total Time:** 16 Minutes | **Calories:** 176 | **Fat:** 14.7 g | **Protein:** 6 g | **Carbs:** 10.5 g | **Fiber:** 4 g

Ingredients and Quantity

- 2 tsp. cumin powder
- 4 garlic cloves, peeled and minced
- 1 small onion, peeled and chopped
- 2 tbsp. bran cereal, crushed
- 18 medium-sized white mushrooms
- Fine sea salt and freshly ground black pepper, to your taste
- A pinch ground allspice
- 2 tbsp. olive oil

Direction

1. First, clean the mushrooms; remove the middle stalks from the mushrooms to prepare the "shells".
2. Grab a mixing dish and thoroughly combine the remaining items.
3. Fill the mushrooms with the prepared mixture.
4. Cook the mushrooms at 345 degrees F (180 C) heat for 12 minutes. Enjoy!

Mediterranean Halloumi and Garlic Omelet

Servings: 2 | **Total Time:** 17 Minutes | **Calories:** 444 | **Fat:** 29 g | **Protein:** 30 g | **Carbs:** 11.6 g | **Fiber:** 2 g

Ingredients and Quantity

- 1/3 cup vegan Halloumi cheese, sliced
- 2 tsp. garlic paste
- 2 tsp. fresh chopped rosemary
- 1 ¼ applesauce
- 2 bell peppers, seeded and chopped
- 1 ½ tbsp. fresh basil, chopped
- 3 tbsp. onions, chopped
- Fine sea salt and ground black pepper, to taste

Direction

1. Spritz your baking dish with a canola cooking spray.
2. Throw in all ingredients and stir until everything is well incorporated.
3. Bake for about 15 minutes at 325 degrees F (163 C). Eat warm. Enjoy!

Roma Tomato Bites with Halloumi Cheese

Servings: 4 | **Total Time:** 20 Minutes | **Calories:** 428 | **Fat:** 38.4 g | **Protein:** 18.8 g | **Carbs:** 4.5 g | **Fiber:** 2.2 g

Ingredients and Quantity

For the Sauce:

- 1/3 cup extra-virgin olive oil
- ½ cup Parmigiano-Reggiano cheese, grated
- 1 tsp. garlic puree
- ½ tsp. fine sea salt
- 4 tbsp. pecans, chopped

For the Tomato Bites:

- 2 large sized Roma tomatoes, cut into thin slices and pat them dry
- 8 oz. Halloumi cheese, cut into thin slices
- 1 tsp. dried basil
- ¼ tsp. red pepper flakes, crushed
- 1/8 tsp. sea salt
- 1/3 cup onions, sliced

Direction

1. Start by preheating your air fryer to 380 F (193 C).
2. Make the sauce by mixing all ingredients, except the extra-virgin olive oil, in your food processor.
3. While the machine is running, slowly and gradually pour in the olive oil; puree until everything is well - blended.
4. Now, spread 1 teaspoon of the sauce over the top of each tomato slice.
5. Place a slice of Halloumi cheese on each tomato slice.
6. Top with onion slices. Sprinkle with basil, red pepper, and sea salt.
7. Transfer the bites to the Air Fryer basket.
8. Drizzle with olive oil and cook for approximately 14 minutes.
9. Arrange these bites on a nice serving platter, garnish with the remaining sauce and serve at room temperature. Enjoy!

Indian-Style Garnet Sweet Potatoes

Servings: 4 | **Total Time:** 24 Minutes | **Calories:** 103 | **Fat:** 9.1 g | **Protein:** 1.9 g | **Carbs:** 4.9 g | **Fiber:** 1.2 g

Ingredients and Quantity

- 1/3 tsp. white pepper
- 1 tbsp. coconut oil
- ½ tsp. turmeric powder
- 5 garnet sweet potatoes, peeled and diced
- 1 ½ tbsp. maple syrup
- 2 tsp. tamarind paste
- 1 ½ tbsp. fresh lime juice
- 1 ½ tsp. ground allspice

Direction

1. In a mixing bowl, toss all ingredients until sweet potatoes are well coated.
2. Air-fry them at 335 degrees F (168 C) for 12 minutes.
3. Pause the air fryer and toss again.
4. Increase the temperature to 390 degrees F (200 C) and cook for an additional 10 minutes. Eat warm. Enjoy!

Easy Sautéed Green Beans

Servings: 4 | **Total Time:** 12 Minutes | **Calories:** 53 | **Fat:** 3 g | **Protein:** 1.6 g | **Carbs:** 6.1 g | **Fiber:** 1.2 g

Ingredients and Quantity

- ¾ pound green beans, cleaned
- 1 tbsp. balsamic vinegar
- ¼ tsp. kosher salt
- ½ tsp. mixed peppercorns, freshly cracked
- 1 tbsp. coconut oil
- Sesame seeds, to serve

Direction

1. Set your air fryer to cook at 390 F (200 C).
2. Mix the green beans with all of the above ingredients, apart from the sesame seeds.
3. Set the timer for 10 minutes.
4. Meanwhile, toast the sesame seeds in a small-sized nonstick skillet; make sure to stir continuously.
5. Serve sautéed green beans on a nice serving platter sprinkled with toasted sesame seeds. Enjoy!

Easy Cheesy Cauliflower and Broccoli

Servings: 6 | **Total Time:** 20 Minutes | **Calories:** 133 | **Fat:** 9.5 g | **Protein:** 5.9 g | **Carbs:** 9.5 g | **Fiber:** 3.2 g

Ingredients and Quantity

- 1 pound cauliflower florets
- 1 pound broccoli florets
- 2 ½ tbsp. sesame oil
- 1/2 tsp. smoked cayenne pepper
- ¾ tsp. sea salt flakes
- 1 tbsp. lemon zest, grated
- ½ cup Violife cheese, shredded

Direction

1. Prepare the cauliflower and broccoli using your favorite steaming method.
2. Then, drain them well; add the sesame oil, cayenne pepper, and salt flakes.
3. Air-fry at 390 degrees F (200 C) for approximately 16 minutes; make sure to check the vegetables halfway through the cooking time.
4. Afterwards, stir in the lemon zest and Violife cheese.
5. Toss to coat well and serve immediately!

Greek-Style Mushrooms

Servings: 2 | **Total Time:** 32 Minutes | **Calories:** 60 | **Fat:** 8 g | **Protein:** 5 g | **Carbs:** 2 g | **Fiber:** 0.7 g

Ingredients and Quantity

- 5 tsp. lemon juice
- 2 bay leaves
- 1 tsp. coriander seeds
- 1 tsp. black pepper
- 700 g mushrooms
- 4 tsp. minced parsley
- Salt, to taste

Direction

1. Add a liter of water in a saucepan with lemon juice, bay leaves, coriander seeds, and black pepper. Season with salt.
2. Wait till it boils and cook in the air fryer at 350 F (180 C) for 10 minutes.
3. Remove the grounded part of the champignon's feet. Wash quickly, drain and cut into pieces.
4. Add the mushrooms to the pan and wait for it to boil again.
5. Set 2 minutes and turn off the heat.
6. Add the parsley. Mix gently. Let it cool completely in the broth.
7. Drain the mushrooms, put them on a plate, and drizzle with the cooking broth, adding some coriander grains. Serve and enjoy!

Lentil Fritters

Prep Time: 15 Minutes | **Cooking Time:** 12 Minutes | **Servings:** 9 | **Calories:** 49 | **Carbs:** 9 g | **Protein:** 3 g | **Fat:** 0.4 g | **Sugar:** 1.1 g | **Sodium:** 84 mg | **Fibre:** 2.3 g

Ingredients and Quantity

- 1 cup cooked red lentils
- 1 cup riced cauliflower
- ½ medium zucchini, shredded (about 1 cup)
- ¼ cup finely chopped onion
- ¼ tsp. salt
- ¼ tsp. black pepper
- ½ tsp. garlic powder
- ¼ tsp. paprika
- ¼ cup applesauce
- 1/3 cup quinoa flour

Direction

1. Preheat the air fryer to 370 F (190 C).
2. In a large bowl, mix the lentils, cauliflower, zucchini, onion, salt, pepper, garlic powder. Mix in the applesauce and flour until a thick dough forms.
3. Using a large spoon, form the dough into 9 large fritters.
4. Liberally spray the air fryer basket with olive oil. Place the fritters into the basket, leaving space around each fritter so you can flip them.
5. Cook for 6 minutes, flip, and cook for another 6 minutes.

6. Remove from the air fryer and repeat with the remaining fritters. Serve warm with desired sauce and sides. Enjoy!

Veggie Fried Rice

Prep Time: 10 Minutes | **Cooking Time:** 25 Minutes | **Servings:** 4 | **Calories:** 140 | **Carbs:** 16 g | **Protein:** 5.7 g | **Fat:** 6.3 g | **Sugar:** 2.7 g | **Sodium:** 704 mg | **Fibre:** 1.6 g

Ingredients and Quantity

- 1 cup cooked brown rice
- 1/3 cup chopped onion
- ½ cup chopped carrots
- ½ chopped carrots
- ½ cup chopped bell peppers
- ½ cup chopped broccoli florets
- 3 tbsp. low-sodium soy sauce
- 1 tbsp. sesame oil
- 1 tsp. ground ginger
- 1 tsp. ground garlic powder
- ½ tsp. black pepper
- 1/8 tsp. salt
- ½ cup applesauce

Direction

1. Preheat the air fryer to 370 F (190 C).
2. In a large bowl, mix together the brown rice, onions, carrots, bell pepper, and broccoli.
3. In a small bowl, whisk together the soy sauce, sesme oil, ginger, garlic powder, pepper, salt, and applesauce.
4. Pour the small bowl mixture into the rice and vegetable mixture, and then mix together.
5. Liberally spray a 7-inch springform (or compatible air fryer dish) with olive oil. Add the rice mixture to the pan and cover with aluminium foil.
6. Place a metal trivet into the air fryer basket and set the pan on top. Cook for 15 minutes.
7. Carefully remove the pan from the basket, discard the foil, and mix the rice.
8. Return the rice to the air fryer basket, turning down the temperature to 350 F (180 C) and cooking for another 10 minutes.
9. Remove and let cool for 5 minutes. Serve warm. Enjoy!

Mexican-Style Roasted Corn

Prep Time: 10 Minutes | **Cooking Time:** 14 Minutes | **Servings:** 3 | **Calories:** 227 | **Carbs:** 20 g | **Protein:** 4.6 g | **Fat:** 10.8 g | **Sugar:** 4 g | **Sodium:** 294 mg | **Fibre:** 1.9 g

Ingredients and Quantity

- 3 tbsp. coconut oil, melted and cooled
- 2 tsp. minced garlic
- ¾ tsp. ground cumin
- ¾ tsp. red pepper flakes
- ¼ tsp. table salt
- 3 cold 4-inch lengths husked and de-silked corn on the cob
- Fresh cilantro leaves, minced
- Queso Fresco, crumbled

Direction

1. Preheat the air fryer to 400 F (205 C).
2. Mix the coconut oil, garlic, cumin, red pepper flakes, and salt in a large zip-closed plastic bag.
3. Add the cold corn pieces, seal the bag, and massage the butter into the surface of the corn.
4. When the machine is at temperature, take the pieces of corn out of the plastic bag and put them in the basket, with as much air space between the pieces as possible.

5. Air-fry undisturbed for 14 minutes, until golden brown, and maybe even charred in a few small spots.
6. Use kitchen tongs to gently transfer the pieces of corn to a serving platter.
7. Sprinkle each with the cilantro and quso fresco. Serve warm. Enjoy!

Roasted Vegetable Frittata

Prep Time: 10 Minutes | **Cooking Time:** 19 Minutes | **Servings:** 1 | **Calories:** 528 | **Carbs:** 9.2 g | **Protein:** 34.3 g | **Fat:** 10.8 g | **Sugar:** 5 g | **Sodium:** 84 mg | **Fibre:** 2.6 g

Ingredients and Quantity

- ½ red or green bell pepper, cut into ½ inch chunks
- 4 button mushrooms, sliced
- ½ cup diced zucchini
- ½ tsp. chopped fresh oregano or thyme
- 1 tsp. olive oil
- ¾ cups applesauce
- ½ cup grated cheddar cheese
- Salt and freshly ground black pepper, to taste
- 1 tsp. coconut oil
- 1 tsp. chopped fresh parsley

Direction

1. Preheat the air fryer to 400 F (205 C).
2. Toss the pepper, mushrooms, zucchini and oregano with the olive oil, and then air-fry for 6 minutes, shaking the basket once or twice during the cooking process to redistribute the ingredients.
3. While the vegetables are cooking, pour the applesauce in a bowl, stir in the Cheddar cheese and season with salt and freshly ground black pepper.
4. Add the air-fried vegetables to this bowl when they have finished cooking.
5. Place a 6 or 7-inch non-stick metal cake pan into the air fryer basket using an aluminium sling to lower the pan into the basket. Fold a piece of aluminium foil into a strip about 2-inches wide by 24-inches long.
6. Air-fry at 380 F (193 C) for 12 minutes, or until the frittata has puffed up and is lightly browned. Let the frittata sit in the air fryer for 5 minutes to cool to an edible temperature and set up.
7. Remove the cake pan from the air fryer, sprinkle with parsley and serve immediately. Enjoy!

Sweet Potato-Cinnamon Toast

Prep Time: 10 Minutes | **Cooking Time:** 8 Minutes | **Servings:** 6 | **Calories:** 39 | **Carbs:** 4.5 g | **Protein:** 0.4 g | **Fat:** 2.3 g | **Sugar:** 1.3 g | **Sodium:** 7 mg | **Fibre:** 0.9 g

Ingredients and Quantity

- 1 small sweet potato, cut into 3/8-inch slices
- Oil, for misting
- Ground cinnamon

Direction

1. Preheat air fryer to 390 F (200 C).
2. Spray both sides of the potato slices with oil. Sprinkle both sides with cinnamon to taste.
3. Place the potato slices in air fryer basket in a single layer.
4. Cook for 4 minutes, turn, and cook for 4 more minutes, or until the potato slices are barely fork tender. Serve and enjoy!

Crisp Banana Chips

Servings: 2 | **Total Time:** 18 Minutes

Ingredients and Quantity

- 1 large-sized plantain banana
- 1 tsp. coconut oil
- ½ tsp. salt
- ¼ tsp. turmeric powder
- Pinch chili powder

Direction

1. Preheat the air fryer to 190 C (375 F).
2. Peel the plantain and cut it into thin round pieces - do not slice them into wafer thin pieces, otherwise, the chips will fly into the coils when they begin to get crispy.
3. Put the plantain slices into a bowl and toss with the turmeric powder and coconut oil.
4. Transfer to the air fryer basket and set the timer for 7 to 8 minutes, removing and shaking the basket every 2 minutes. The chips are done when they are crisp and light golden brown.
5. When the chips are cooked, let them cool 2 minutes or more to allow them to get crisper. Serve and enjoy!

Crumbed Tempeh

Servings: 2 | **Total Time:** 17 Minutes

Ingredients and Quantity

- 200 g packet tempeh
- 3 to 4 tbsp. Besan flour
- ½ tsp. celery salt
- 1 tsp. smoked paprika
- ½ cup Panko breadcrumbs
- Almond milk

Direction

1. Slice up the tempeh in 1cm strips.
2. Mix the Besan flour, celery salt and paprika.
3. Dip the tempeh strip into the almond milk then coat with the flour mix.
4. Put the tempeh back into the milk and then coat with the breadcrumbs.
5. Sprinkle a little extra celery salt and cook at 180 degrees Celsius (350 F) for 12 minutes. Serve and enjoy!

Buffalo Tofu

Servings: 2 | **Total Time:** 1 Hour 20 Minutes

Ingredients and Quantity

- 1 block extra-firm tofu, drained and pressed
- 1 cup vegan hot sauce
- ¼ cup vegan butter, melted

For Serving:

- Vegan ranch or blue cheese dressing

Direction

1. Cut the tofu into squares.
2. Preheat the air fryer to 390 degrees Fahrenheit (200 C).

3. Whisk the hot sauce with the melted butter to form the buffalo sauce.
4. Marinate the tofu in the buffalo sauce mixture for 30 - 60 minutes.
5. Once the air fryer is preheated, coat the basket lightly with cooking oil spray and using tongs, add the tofu to the air fryer basket. Reserve the marinade.
6. Air-fry for 20 - 30 minutes, checking and shaking the tofu after 10 minutes, and then each additional 5 minutes after that.
7. Check the tofu each time for the desired crispness.
8. Toss the tofu back into the reserved hot sauce and then transfer to a serving plate.
9. If desired, serve alongside vegan blue cheese or ranch dressing. Enjoy!

Dinner Recipes

Pepper Jack Cauliflower Bites

Servings: 2 | **Total Time:** 24 Minutes | **Calories:** 271 | **Fat:** 23 g | **Protein:** 9.8 g | **Carbs:** 8.9 g | **Fiber:** 2.8 g

Ingredients and Quantity

- 1/3 tsp. shallot powder
- 1 tsp. ground black pepper
- ¼ tsp. cumin powder
- ½ tsp. garlic salt
- 1 ½ large-sized heads of cauliflower, broken into florets
- ¼ cup pepper Jack cheese, grated
- 1 ½ tbsp. vegetable oil
- 1/3 tsp. paprika

Direction

1. Boil cauliflower in a large pan of salted water approximately 5 minutes.
2. After that, drain the cauliflower florets; now, transfer them to a baking dish.
3. Toss the cauliflower florets with the rest of the above ingredients.
4. Roast at 395 degrees F (200 C) for 16 minutes, turn them halfway through the process. Enjoy!

Mint-Butter Stuffed Mushrooms

Servings: 3 | **Total Time:** 20 Minutes | **Calories:** 290 | **Fat:** 14.7 g | **Protein:** 28 g | **Carbs:** 13.4 g | **Fiber:** 3.3 g

Ingredients and Quantity

- 3 garlic cloves, minced
- 1 tsp. ground black pepper, or more, to taste
- 1/3 cup seasoned breadcrumbs
- 1 ½ tbsp. fresh mint, chopped
- 1 tsp. salt, or more, to taste
- 1 ½ tbsp. coconut oil
- 14 medium-sized mushrooms, cleaned, stalks removed

Direction

1. Mix all of the above ingredients, minus the mushrooms, in a mixing bowl to prepare the filling.
2. Then, stuff the mushrooms with the prepared filling.
3. Air-fry stuffed mushrooms at 375 degrees F (190 C) for about 12 minutes.
4. Taste for doneness and serve at room temperature as a vegetarian appetizer. Enjoy!

Gorgonzola Stuffed Mushrooms with Horseradish Mayo

Servings: 5 | **Total Time:** 15 Minutes | **Calories:** 210 | **Fat:** 15.2 g | **Protein:** 7.6 g | **Carbs:** 13.6 g | **Fiber:** 2.7 g

Ingredients and Quantity

- ½ cup breadcrumbs
- 2 garlic cloves, pressed

- 2 tbsp. fresh coriander, chopped
- 1/3 tsp. kosher salt
- ½ tsp. crushed red pepper flakes
- 1 ½ tbsp. olive oil
- 20 medium-sized mushrooms, cut off the stems
- ½ cup vegan Gorgonzola cheese, grated
- ¼ cup low fat vegan mayonnaise
- 1 tsp. prepared horseradish, well drained
- 1 tbsp. fresh parsley, finely chopped

Direction

1. Mix the breadcrumbs together with the garlic, coriander, salt, red pepper, and the olive oil; mix to combine well.
2. Stuff the mushroom caps with the breadcrumb filling.
3. Top with grated Gorgonzola.
4. Place the mushrooms in the Air Fryer grill pan and slide them into the machine.
5. Grill them at 380 degrees F (193 C) for 8 to 12 minutes or until the stuffing is warmed through.
6. Meanwhile, prepare the horseradish mayo by mixing the mayonnaise, horseradish and parsley.
7. Serve with the warm fried mushrooms. Enjoy!

Orange Tofu

Servings: 4 | **Total Time:** 40 Minutes | **Calories:** 109 | **Fat:** 3 g | **Protein:** 8 g | **Carbs:** 11 g | **Fiber:** 2 g

Ingredients and Quantity

For the Tofu:

- 1 lb. extra-firm tofu, drained and pressed
- 1 tbsp. tamari
- 1 tbsp. cornstarch or arrowroot powder

For the Sauce:

- 1 tsp. fresh ginger, minced
- 1 tsp. fresh garlic, minced
- 1 tsp. orange zest
- 1/3 cup orange juice
- ½ cup water
- 2 tsp. cornstarch or arrowroot powder
- 1 tbsp. real maple syrup
- ¼ tsp. red pepper flakes

Direction

1. Cut the tofu into 1-inch cubes.
2. Place the tofu in a Ziploc bag and add the tamari then seal the bag. Shake the bag until all the tofu is well coated with the tamari.
3. Now add the tablespoon of cornstarch to the bag and shake again until all the tofu is coated. Marinate for 15 minutes or more.
4. Now add all the sauce ingredients to a small bowl and mix well.
5. In a single layer, place the tofu into the air fryer and cook the tofu at 390 degrees Fahrenheit (200 C) for 10 minutes, shaking it halfway through cooking. The tofu will probably need to be cooked in batches to avoid uneven cooking.
6. Once done, add the tofu to a skillet on the stove top over a medium-high heat.
7. Stir the sauce and pour it over the tofu until the sauce is thick and glossy and the tofu is heated through.
8. Serve immediately with rice, noodles and steamed vegetables, if desired. Enjoy!

Golden Turmeric Cauliflower Steaks

Servings: 2 | **Total Time:** 25 Minutes

Ingredients and Quantity

- 1 to 2 medium heads cauliflower, stems intact
- 2 tbsp. coconut oil or coconut spray oil
- 1 tsp. ground turmeric
- ¼ tsp. ground ginger
- 1/8 tsp. ground cumin
- 1/8 tsp. salt
- A pinch black pepper

For Serving:

- Mixed steamed greens
- Tahini
- White sesame seeds

Direction

1. Cut the cauliflower head down the middle, leaving the stem intact. Trim off any green leaves.
2. On either side of the half, cut 1-inch steaks taking care not to make them too thin. Reserve any fallen florets for use at a later date.
3. Coat the steaks with coconut oil or coconut oil spray and rub the spices into all of the cracks and crevices of the cauliflower.
4. This recipes can be prepared in the oven or in an air fryer. Cook at 390 degrees Fahrenheit (200 C) for about 15 minutes, turning over the steaks halfway through the cooking time.
5. Serve on a bed of mixed greens drizzled with tahini.
6. Garnish with white sesame seeds, if desired. Enjoy!

Portobello Mushrooms with Hummus Sauce

Servings: 4 | **Total Time:** 25 Minutes | **Calories:** 70 | **Fat:** 1.6 g | **Protein:** 4.3 g | **Carbs:** 11 g | **Fiber:** 3.5 g

Ingredients and Quantity

- 4 large Portobello mushrooms
- 4 tbsp. oil-free pasta sauce
- 1 garlic clove, minced
- 2 tbsp. red bell pepper, diced
- ½ cup hummus
- 3 oz. zucchini, grated
- 4 olives Kalamata olives, pitted and sliced
- 1 tsp. dried basil
- Balsamic vinegar
- Salt and black pepper, to taste
- Fresh basil leaves or other herbs, finely chopped

Direction

1. Wash the Portobello mushrooms, cut off the stems and remove the grills. Pat the insides dry and brush both sides with balsamic vinegar.
2. Season the mushrooms with salt and pepper.
3. Spread 1 tablespoon of the pasta sauce inside each mushroom and sprinkle with the chopped garlic.
4. Preheat the air fryer to 330 degrees Fahrenheit (165 C).
5. Place the mushrooms in a single layer and cook for 3 minutes.
6. Remove the mushrooms and top each with equal portions of peppers, zucchini and olives and sprinkle with dried basil, salt and pepper.
7. Return the mushrooms to the air fryer and cook for 3 more minutes.
8. Check the mushrooms after 3 minutes and return to the air fryer for another 3 minutes or until mushrooms are tender.
9. Place on a plate, drizzle with hummus and sprinkle with the fresh basil or any other herb of your choice. Serve immediately. Enjoy!

Crispy Brussels Sprouts

Prep Time: 10 Minutes | **Cooking Time:** 12 Minutes | **Servings:** 3 | **Calories:** 142 | **Carbs:** 14.6 g | **Protein:** 6.4 g | **Fat:** 7.6 g | **Sugar:** 4.1 g | **Sodium:** 626 mg | **Fibre:** 3.1 g

Ingredients and Quantity

- 1 ¼ pounds medium, 2-inch in length Brussels sprouts
- 1 ½ tbsp. olive oil
- ¾ tsp. table salt

Direction

1. Preheat the air fryer to 400 F (205 C).
2. Halve each Brussels sprout through the stem end, pulling off and discarding any discolored outer leaves. Put the sprout halves in a large bowl, add the oil and salt, and stir well to coat evenly, until the Brussels sprouts are glistening.
3. When the machine is at temperature, scrape the contents of the bowl into the basket, gently spreading the Brussels sprout halves into as close to one layer as possible.
4. Air-fry for 12 minutes, gently tossing and rearranging the vegetables twice to get all covered or touching parts exposed to the air currents, until crisp and browned at the edges.
5. Gently pour the contents of the basket onto a wire rack. Cool for a minute or two before serving. Enjoy!

Mediterranean-Style Frittata with Manchego

Servings: 4 | **Total Time:** 40 Minutes | **Calories:** 153 | **Fat:** 11.9 g | **Protein:** 9.3 g | **Carbs:** 3.2 g | **Fiber:** 1.7 g

Ingredients and Quantity

- 1/3 cup grated Manchego cheese
- 1 ¼ applesauce
- 1 small onion, finely chopped
- 2 garlic, peeled and finely minced
- 1 ½ cups white mushrooms, chopped
- 1 tsp. dried basil
- 1 ½ tbsp. olive oil
- ¾ tsp. dried oregano
- ½ tsp. dried parsley flakes or 1 tbsp. fresh flat leaf Italian parsley
- 1 tsp. porcini powder
- Table salt and freshly ground black pepper, to savor

Direction

1. Start by preheating your air fryer to 350 degrees F (180 C).
2. Add the oil, mushrooms, onion, and green garlic to the air fryer baking dish.
3. Bake this mixture for 6 minutes or until it is tender.
4. Meanwhile, pour the applesuace into a small bowl. Next, add the seasonings and mix well.
5. Pause your air fryer and take the baking dish out of the air fryer.
6. Pour the applesauce mixture into the baking dish with sautéed mixture.
7. Top with the grated Manchego.
8. Bake for about 32 minutes at 320 degrees F (160 C) or until your frittata is set.
9. Serve warm garnished with diced fresh tomatoes. Enjoy!

Toasted Coconut French Toast

Servings: 1 | **Total Time:** 9 Minutes

Ingredients and Quantity

- 2 slices gluten-free bread
- ½ cup unsweetened shredded coconut
- ½ cup unsweetened coconut milk
- 1 tsp. baking powder

Direction

1. In a wide rimmed shallow bowl, mix the coconut milk and baking powder and set aside.
2. In another shallow bowl, spread the shredded coconut out into an even layer.
3. Take each slice of the gluten-free bread and soak it in the coconut milk mixture for a few seconds.
4. Transfer the soaked slice to the shredded coconut bowl and fully coat the slice in the shredded coconut.
5. Carefully place both slices of the coconut bread in your air fryer and close.
6. Cook at 350 degrees Fahrenheit (180 C) for 4 minutes.
7. Once done, remove and top with maple syrup or your favorite topping. Enjoy!

Pecan French Toast

Servings: 12 | **Total Time:** 20 Minutes

Ingredients and Quantity

- 8 pieces whole-grain, gluten-free, vegan bread
- 1 cup rolled oats
- 1 cup pecans, (or any other nut of your choice)
- 2 tbsp. ground flax seed
- ¾ cup almond milk (plain or vanilla-flavored)
- 1 tsp. ground cinnamon

For Serving:

- Real maple syrup

Direction

1. Make the topping for the toast by mixing the flaxseeds, oats, pecans and ground cinnamon to a food processor and pulse until the mixture resembles coarse bread crumbs.
2. Pour into a shallow bowl that's large enough to dip in the bread slices.
3. Add the almond milk to a medium-sized bowl and then briefly soak one or two pieces of the bread for 15 seconds, then flip over and soak the other side. Be careful that the bread does not become mushy.
4. Place the amount of slices that fit into the air fryer basket in a single layer and cook at 350 degrees Fahrenheit (180 C) for 3 minutes, then flip the bread over and cook for a further 3 minutes.
5. Repeat until all the bread slices are done.
6. Top with maple syrup or any other toppings of your choice and enjoy!

Oatmeal with Raspberries

Servings: 2 | **Total Time:** 20 Minutes

Ingredients and Quantity

- 3 oz. oatmeal
- 2 ripe bananas, peeled and mashed
- 1 cup almond milk
- 4 oz. frozen raspberries
- 1/8 tsp. salt

Direction

1. Preheat the air fryer at 350 degrees Fahrenheit or an oven to 400 degrees Fahrenheit (205 C).
2. Using a fork, mash the bananas in a ceramic oven-proof dish and then add then oatmeal, milk and salt.
3. Stir well to mix and then add the frozen raspberries mixing through well.
4. Cook in the air fryer or oven for 15 minutes.
5. Slice and serve immediately, topped with yoghurt and maple syrup!

Corn Muffins

Servings: 12 | **Total Time:** 17 Minutes

Ingredients and Quantity

- 1 packet corn mix
- ¼ cup flax egg
- 1/3 cup almond milk

Direction

1. In a medium-sized bowl mix the corn mix, flax egg and almond milk until smooth.
2. Pour the muffin mix into a greased muffin tin or muffin silicone holders, and air fry at 320 degrees Fahrenheit (160 C), for 12 minutes.
3. When done, serve immediately, warm and enjoy!

Avocado Fries

Servings: 3 | **Total Time:** 20 Minutes

Ingredients and Quantity

- 1 Hass avocado, peeled, pitted and sliced
- ½ cup panko breadcrumbs
- ½ tsp. salt
- Aquafaba from 1 can (15 oz.) garbanzo beans or white beans

Direction

1. Put the salt and panko breadcrumbs into a shallow bowl and toss to mix.
2. Dredge the slices of avocado in the aquafaba and then coat with the panko mixture, covering them evenly well.
3. In a single layer, arrange the coated slices in the air fryer basket – DO NOT OVERLAP.
4. Set the temperature to 390 F (200 C) and the timer for 10 minutes. Shake well after 5 minutes.
5. Serve right away with your favorite vegan dipping sauce. Enjoy!

Corn Tortilla Chips

Servings: 2 | **Total Time:** 4 Minutes

Ingredients and Quantity

- 8 corn tortillas
- 1 tbsp. olive oil
- Salt, to taste

Direction

1. Preheat the air fryer to 200 C (390 F).
2. Using a sharp knife, slice the corn tortillas into triangles.
3. Brush all the triangles with the olive oil.
4. Put half the tortilla pieces in the air fryer basket and set the timer for 3 minutes.
5. Repeat the process with the remaining half.
6. Sprinkle the cooked tortilla with the salt.
7. Serve with salsa, guacamole, or your preferred dip. Enjoy!

Crispy Vegetable Fries

Servings: 4 | **Total Time:** 23 Minutes

Ingredients and Quantity

- 1 cup panko breadcrumbs (regular or gluten-free)
- 1 cup rice flour
- 2 tbsp. vegan egg powder (I used Follow Your Heart)
- 2 tbsp. nutritional yeast flakes, divided
- 2/3 cup cold water
- Assorted veggies of your choice, sliced into shapes similar to French fry or into bite-size chunks (such as green beans, cauliflower, zucchini, sweet onions or squash)
- Salt and pepper

Direction

1. Prepare 3 pieces of shallow dishes on a counter.
2. Put rice flour in one of the dishes.
3. In the second dish, whisk the egg powder with 2/3 cup water and 1 tbsp. nutritional yeast until the mixture is smooth.
4. In the third dish, mix the panko breadcrumbs with the remaining 1 tbsp. nutritional yeast and then add a couple pinches of pepper and salt.
5. Working one vegetable piece at a time, coat with rice flour, into the vegan egg mixture, and finally in the breadcrumb mix, pressing to set the coating. Prepare as many veggies as you desire.
6. Lightly spritz the air fryer with oil.
7. Alternatively, you can line the air fryer basket with parchment paper that is smaller than the basket.
8. Carefully put the coated veggies in the air fryer basket and gently spritz with oil.
9. Set the temperature to 380 F (193 C) and the timer for 8 minutes.
10. Cook for additional minutes, if needed.
11. Serve while still crispy and hot with your choice of dipping sauce. Enjoy!

Buffalo Cauliflower

Servings: 4 | **Total Time:** 30 Minutes

Ingredients and Quantity

For the Cauliflower:

- 4 cups cauliflower - use florets that are in the size of 2 pieces baby carrots put side-by-side
- 1 cup panko breadcrumbs
- 1 tsp. sea salt - Do not use regular salt

For the Buffalo Coating:

- ¼ cup vegan Buffalo sauce (I used Frank's Red Hot) - check the ingredients for butter
- ¼ cup vegan butter, melted measurement

For Dipping:

- Vegan mayo cashew ranch, or your favorite creamy salad dressing

Direction

1. Put the vegan butter in a microwavable mug and microwave to melt. Add the buffalo sauce and whisk to combine.
2. Combine the panko breadcrumbs with the salt in a shallow bowl.
3. Hold a floret by the stem, dip into the Buffalo coating, making sure that the floret is coated with the sauce – it's perfectly fine if the stem isn't coated with the sauce.
4. Hold the floret over the mug until the sauce stops dripping from it – few drips are okay, but the raining sauce is not since it will make the panko bread clumpy and stop sticking on the cauliflower.
5. Dredge the sauce-coated floret in the breadcrumb mixture, coating it as much as you like, and then put into the air fryer basket.
6. Repeat the process with the remaining florets – no need to arrange them in a single layer in the basket, just put them in.
7. Set the temperature to 350 F (180 C) and set the timer for 14-17 minutes, shaking the basket a couple of times and checking the progress during the process. The cauliflower is cooked when the florets are browned a little bit.
8. Serve with your choice of dipping sauce. Enjoy!

Cauliflower Chickpea Tacos

Servings: 4 | **Total Time:** 30 Minutes

Ingredients and Quantity

- 19 oz. can chickpeas, drained and rinsed
- 4 cups cauliflower florets, cut into bite-sized pieces
- 2 tbsp. taco seasoning
- 2 tbsp. olive oil

For Serving:

- 8 small flour tortillas
- 4 cups cabbage, finely shredded
- 2 Haas avocados, sliced
- Coconut yogurt, for drizzling

Direction

1. Pre-heat the air fryer to 390 degrees Fahrenheit (200 C).
2. In a large bowl, toss the chickpeas and cauliflower with taco seasoning and olive oil.
3. Put them into the basket of the air fryer and cook in the air fryer for 20 minutes. Make sure to check occasionally to ensure the cauliflower and chickpeas are evenly cooked through.
4. Serve in tacos with the cabbage, avocado slices, and coconut yogurt drizzled on top. Enjoy!

Rainbow Veggies

Servings: 4 | **Total Time:** 30 Minutes | **Calories:** 69 | **Fat:** 3.8 g | **Protein:** 2.6 g | **Carbs:** 7.7 g | **Fiber:** 2.5 g

Ingredients and Quantity

- 1 zucchini, finely diced
- 1 red bell pepper, seeded and diced
- 1 yellow summer squash, finely diced
- ½ sweet white onion, finely diced
- 4 oz. fresh mushrooms, cleaned and halved
- 1 tbsp. extra-virgin olive oil
- Salt and pepper, to taste

Direction

1. Preheat the air fryer according to the recommendations of the air fryer.
2. Place the red bell pepper, zucchini, mushrooms, squash and onion in a large bowl.
3. Add the olive oil, black pepper and salt, and toss to combine.
4. Place the vegetables in a single layer in the air fryer basket.
5. Air-fry the vegetables for 20 minutes, stirring halfway through the cooking time. Serve and enjoy!

BONUS: VEGAN AND VEGETARIAN AIR FRYER DESSERT RECIPES FOR SPECIAL SEASONS

Special seasons are seasons for merriment and relaxation. Here are some delicious vegan and vegetarian air fryer desert recipes to help you celebrate these special seasons without going off the vegan and vegetarian track.

Apple Hand Pies

Prep Time: 15 Minutes | **Cooking Time:** 23 Minutes | **Servings:** 6 | **Calories:** 284 | **Fat:** 16 g | **Carbs:** 31.6 g | **Protein:** 3.7 g

Ingredients and Quantity

- 8 tbsp. almond butter, softened
- 12 tbsp. brown sugar
- 2 tbsp. cinnamon, ground
- 4 medium Granny Smith apples, diced
- 2 tsp. almond flour
- 4 tsp. cold water
- 1 (400 g) package pastry, 9-inch crust pie
- Non-stick cooking spray
- 1 tbsp. grapeseed oil
- 100 g powdered sugar
- 2 tsp. almond milk

Direction

1. Preheat the air fryer to 200 C (390 F).
2. Toss apples with brown sugar, butter, and cinnamon in a suitable frying pan.
3. Set this frying pan over medium heat and stir cook for 5 minutes.
4. Mix corn flour with cold water in a small bowl.
5. Add corn flour mixture into the apple and cook for 1 minute until it thickens.
6. Remove this filling from the heat and allow it to cool.
7. Unroll the pie crust and spray on a floured surface.
8. Cut the dough into 16 equal rectangles.
9. Wet the edges of the 8 rectangles with water and divide the apple filling at the centre of these rectangles.
10. Place the other 8 rectangles on top and crimp the edges with a fork, then make 2-3 slashes on top.
11. Place the small pies in the Air Fryer Basket.
12. Return the Air Fryer Basket to the Air Fryer and cook for 17 minutes at 200 C (390 F).
13. Flip the pies once cooked halfway through, and resume cooking.
14. Meanwhile, mix sugar with milk.
15. Pour this mixture over the apple pies. Serve fresh. Enjoy!

Biscuit Doughnuts

Prep Time: 10 Minutes | **Cooking Time:** 15 Minutes | **Servings:** 6 | **Calories:** 192 | **Fat:** 9.3 g | **Carbs:** 27.1 g | **Protein:** 3.2 g

Ingredients and Quantity

- 100 g white sugar
- 1 tsp. cinnamon
- 100 g powdered sugar
- 1 can pre-made bisuit dough
- Coconut oil
- Melted butter, to brush the bisuits

Direction

1. Preheat your air fryer to 190 C (375 F).
2. Place all the biscuits on a cutting board and cut holes in the centre of each biscuit using a cookie cutter.
3. Grease the Air Fryer Basket with coconut oil.
4. Place the biscuits doughnuts in the Air Fryer Basket while keeping them 1 inch apart.
5. Return the Air Fryer Basket to the Air Fryer and cook for 15 minutes at 190 C (375 F).
6. Brush all the doughnuts with melted butter and sprinkle cinnamon and sugar on top.
7. Air fry these doughnuts for one minute more. Serve and enjoy!

Cranberry Scones

Prep Time: 15 Minutes | **Cooking Time:** 16 Minutes | **Servings:** 6 | **Calories:** 204 | **Fat:** 9 g | **Carbs:** 27 g | **Protein:** 1.3 g

Ingredients and Quantity

- 480 g sugar
- 106 g brown sugar
- 2 tbsp. baking powder
- ½ tsp. ground nutmeg
- ½ tsp. salt
- 113 g almond butter, chilled and diced
- 200 g fresh cranberry
- 180 g sugar
- 2 tbsp. orange zest
- 260 g half and half cream
- 2/4 cup flax egg

Direction

1. Prheat the air fryer to 190 C (375 F).
2. Whisk the flour baking powder, salt, nutmeg, and both the sugars in a bowl.
3. Stir in the flax egg and cream, mix well to form a smooth dough.
4. Fold in the cranberries along with the orange zest.
5. Knead this dough well on a work surface.
6. Cut 3-inch circles out of the dough.
7. Place the scones in the air fryer basket and spray them with cooking oil.
8. Return the air fryer basket to the air fryer and cook for 16 minutes at 190 C (375 F).
9. Flip the scones once cooked halfway through and resume cooking. Serve and enjoy!

Apple Nutmeg Flautas

Prep Time: 10 Minutes | **Cooking Time:** 8 Minutes | **Servings:** 6 | **Calories:** 157 | **Fat:** 1.3 g | **Carbs:** 1.3 g | **Protein:** 8.2 g

Ingredients and Quantity

- 55 g light-brown sugar
- 15 g all-purpose flour
- ¼ tsp. ground cinnamon
- Nutmeg, to taste
- 4 apples, peeled, cored and sliced
- ½ lemon, juice and zest
- 6 (10-inch) flour tortillas
- Vegetable oil
- Caramel sauce
- Cinnamon sugar, for garnishing

Direction

1. Preheat the air fryer to 200 C (390 F).

2. Mix the brown sugar with the cinnamon, nutmeg and flour in a large bowl.
3. Toss in apples in lemon juice. Mix well.
4. Place a tortilla at a time on a flat surface and add 1/6 of the apple mixture to the tortilla.
5. Roll the tortilla into a burrito and seal it tightly and hold it in place with a toothpick.
6. Repeat the same ateps with the remaining tortillas and apple mixture.
7. Place the apple burritos in the air fryer basket and spray them with cooking oil.
8. Return the air fryer basket to the air fryer and cook for 8 minutes at 200 C (390 F).
9. Flip the burritos onced cooked halfway through, then resume cooking.
10. Garnish with caramel sauce and cinnamon sugar. Serve and enjoy!

Cheesecake Chimichangas

Prep Time: 15 Minutes | **Cooking Time:** 8 Minutes | **Servings:** 6 | **Calories:** 391 | **Fat:** 24 g | **Carbs:** 38.5 g | **Protein:** 6.6 g

Ingredients and Quantity

- 45 g full-fat coconut milk
- 1 ½ tbsp. granulated sugar
- 1 tsp. vanilla extract
- 8 strawberries, quartered
- 1 banana, peeled and sliced
- 8 flour tortillas
- 8 tsp. Nutella
- Olive oil spray
- 1 (227 g) vegan cream cheese brick, softened
- 3 tbsp. butter, melted

Cinnamon Sugar:

- 2 tbsp. sugar
- 2 tbsp. cinnamon, ground

Direction

1. Beat the cream cheese, coconut milk, vanilla, sugar, strawberries and banana in a bowl.
2. Spread the tortillas on the working surface.
3. Divide the cream mixture onto the tortillas and divide Nutella on top.
4. Roll the tortillas like a burrito and place it in the air fryer basket.
5. Return the air fryer basket to the air fryer and air fry for 8 minutes at 190 C (375 F).
6. Slice the rolls into 1-inch thick pieces and place them on the plate.
7. Drizzle the melted butter and cinnamon sugar on top. Serve and enjoy!

Baked Cinnamon Apples

Prep Time: 10 Minutes | **Cooking Time:** 20 Minutes | **Servings:** 4 | **Calories:** 149 | **Fat:** 1.2 g | **Carbs:** 37.6 g | **Protein:** 1.1 g

Ingredients and Quantity

- 4 apples
- 2 tsp. maple syrup
- 6 tsp. raisins
- 2 tsp. walnuts, chopped
- ½ tsp. cinnamon

Direction

1. Place the apples in a six-inch baking pan.
2. Drizzle maple syrup, raisins, walnuts and cinnamon on top.
3. Place tthe pan in the air fryer basket.
4. Return the air fryer basket to the air fryer.
5. Air fry at 180 C (350 F) for 20 minutes. Serve and enjoy!

Air Fried Brownies

Prep Time: 15 Minutes | **Cooking Time:** 15 Minutes | **Servings:** 6 | **Calories:** 192 | **Fat:** 9.3 g | **Carbs:** 27.1 g | **Protein:** 3.2 g

Ingredients and Quantity

- 60 g all-purpose flour
- 6 tbsp. cocoa powder
- 180 g sugar
- 2 tbsp. almond butter, melted
- 2/4 cup flax egg
- 1 tbsp. vegetable oil
- ½ tsp. vanilla extract
- ¼ tsp. salt
- ¼ tsp. baking powder

Direction

1. Grease a 7-inch baking pan with butter.
2. Preheat the air fryer to 165 C (330 F).
3. Whisk vegetable oil, vanilla extract and butter in a mixing bowl.
4. Stir in cocoa powder, sugar, flax egg, vanilla, flour, salt and baking powder.
5. Mix well until smooth, then pour into the baking pan.
6. Place this pan in the air fryer basket.
7. Return the air fryer basket to the air fryer.
8. Air fry at 165 C (330 F) for 15 minutes. Slice and serve. Enjoy!

Air Fried Churros

Prep Time: 10 Minutes | **Cooking Time:** 12 Minutes | **Servings:** 6 | **Calories:** 204 | **Fat:** 9 g | **Carbs:** 27 g | **Protein:** 1.3 g

Ingredients and Quantity

- 237 ml water
- 75 g butter, cut into cubes
- 2 tbsp. granulated sugar
- ¼ tsp. salt
- 120 g all-purpose flour
- 2/4 cup flax eggs
- 1 tsp. vanilla extract
- Non-stick oil spray

Cinnamon Sugar Coating:

- 100 g granulated sugar
- ¾ tsp. ground cinnamon

Direction

1. Boil water with the sugar, salt and butter in a saucepan over medium-high heat.
2. Reduce heat and add flour, then mix continuously until smooth.
3. Mix the flax egg with vanilla and add to the cooled flour batter.
4. Mix well with a hand mixer until it makes a thick batter.
5. Transfer the mixture to a piping bag.
6. Pipe the mixture on a baking sheet lined with parchment paper into 4 inches long churros.
7. Refrigerate the churros for 1 hour.
8. Place the prepared churros in the air fryer basket and spray them with cooking oil.
9. Return the air fryer basket to the air fryer.
10. Air fry at 190 C (375 F) for 12 minutes.
11. Drizzle sugar and cinnamon on top. Serve and enjoy!

Funnel Cakes

Prep Time: 10 Minutes | **Cooking Time:** 4 Minutes | **Servings:** 6 | **Calories:** 157 | **Fat:** 1.3 g | **Carbs:** 1.3 g | **Protein:** 8.2 g

Ingredients and Quantity

- 120 g all-purpose flour
- 1 ¼ tsp. baking powder
- ¼ tsp. salt
- ½ tsp. ground cinnamon
- 245 g vegan Greek yogurt
- 1 tsp. vanilla extract
- Vegetable oil spray
- Powdered sugar, for serving

Direction

1. Mix ¾ of the flour, salt, cinnamon and baking powder in a bowl.
2. Add vanilla and yogurt, then mix well until it makes a smooth ball.
3. Transfer the prepared dough on a floured surface and roll the dough into a ¼-inch thick sheet.
4. Slice into 1-inch strips and use these strips to make funnel cakes.
5. Place the funnel cakes in the air fryer basket and spray with cooking oil.
6. Return the air fryer basket to the air fryer.
7. Air fry at 190 C (375 F) for 4 minutes.
8. Flip the cakes once cooked halfway through and resume cooking.
9. Serve with powdered sugar on top. Enjoy!

Chocolate Chip Cookies

Prep Time: 15 Minutes | **Cooking Time:** 15 Minutes | **Servings:** 6 | **Calories:** 258 | **Fat:** 12.4 g | **Carbs:** 34.3 g | **Protein:** 3.2 g

Ingredients and Quantity

- 255 g self-rising flour
- 43 g coconut sugar
- 85 g brown sugar
- 142 g almond butter
- 4 tbsp. maple syrup
- 3 tbsp. almond milk
- 1 tbsp. cocoa powder
- 1 tsp. vanilla essence
- 100 g vegan chocolate chips

Direction

1. Preheat the air fryer to 180 C (350 F).
2. Beat the sugars with butter in a mixing bowl using a hand mixer.
3. Stir in milk, vanilla, cocoa powder, maple syrup and flour.
4. Mix well and stir in chocolate chips.
5. Knead the cookie dough and divide it into 12 small cookies.
6. Place the cookies in the air fryer basket, in batches.
7. Return the air fryer basket to the air fryer.
8. Air fry at 180 C (350 F) for 15 minutes.
9. Allow the cookies to cool. Serve and enjoy!

MEAL PREP PLAN GUIDE FOR VEGANS AND VEGETARIANS

The meal plan strategy for vegans and vegetarians is very similar to that of any other diet plan. All you need is to stick to those main rules of a standard meal plan, and you are good to go.

What is Meal Prepping?

Meal prepping is buying fresh ingredients, cleaning/rinsing them, and then preparing them as soon as possible. This makes it easier to create full meals later in the week without having to make everything from scratch. Meal prepping is making homemade lunches, frozen dinners, or instant ramen bowls using fresh, local ingredients but with minimal spending and using only whole food.

This act takes the guesswork and impulse out of your diet. All you need to do is to sit down once in a week and arrange things you will eat throughout a week (this is called meal planning phase) and then prepare and store them ahead of time.

It also saves you the stress of having to cook every single day. You now cook once in a week and still eat healthy meals. This act also goes a long way to help you meet up with your weight loss goal.

Benefits of Meal Prepping

It saves Time

Meal prepping provides loads of free time within the week. Because ingredients for different drinks, meals, or snacks are already sliced and portioned out, these can be cooked or consumed quickly. This is a boon for people with extremely busy schedules.

It saves Money

Saving money on food and groceries becomes easier. The common practice of buying, underutilizing, and throwing out uneaten food in large volumes is extremely wasteful both on one's budget and on the planet's resources. This is evidenced by the numerous limp vegetables in the fridge and the overripe fruits on the kitchen counter that are unlikely to be consumed within the week.

According to a 2015 study in the USA alone, up to $165 billion worth of fresh produce is thrown away yearly. That's 35 million tons of food that is dumped in the landfill. By meal prepping, only ingredients needed for a week's worth of planned meals are to be purchased. This saves almost three-quarters of the usual weekly food budget. This lessens the amount of garbage (from unused food,) and rubbish (from food packaging.)

It Improves Health

By simply creating healthy meals at home, consumption of harmful ingredients from processed food is greatly reduced. These include food additives (e.g. artificial colors and flavors,) preservatives, and overly refined starches. Consumption of salt and sugar is reduced as well.

It also Improves Quality of Meals

More importantly, by buying fresh and whole ingredients only, the quality of consumed food and drinks increase dramatically. Severely limiting the use of processed food or ingredients will boost energy levels.

Common Mistakes to Avoid When Meal Prepping

Meal prepping to lose weight entails energy and time at least for one day per week. It takes a conscious effort from start to finish. However, once a routine is set, meal prepping becomes easier and almost second nature.

To ensure that things start off correctly, try avoiding these mistakes:

Assuming all food and drinks labeled "healthy" are healthy

One of the worst things you can do is to skip the fresh produce section of grocery stores, and buy only processed food and drinks labeled "healthy." Almost all commercially produced "healthy" options (e.g. beverages, frozen dinners, snacks, etc.) are still highly processed and contain inordinately high amounts of food additives, preservatives, refined starches, salt, and sugar. Celebrity-endorsed ones are usually the most expensive too. It is best to remove these from your meal plan.

Whenever possible, opt for fresh ingredients or at least, use less processed ones, like canned or frozen coconut, dried or canned beans, dried or canned mushrooms, dried spices, freeze-dried fruits, frozen vegetables, grains or pseudo grains (e.g. rice, quinoa, wild rice, etc.), packaged green salad mixes, and vinegars.

Limit the use of healthy but highly processed food and drinks, like broth or soup stocks, dark chocolate, energy bars or granola, jams/jellies, kimchi, non-dairy substitutes, peanut butter, pickles, roasted nuts and seeds, sauerkraut, and tomato sauces. If possible, make these from scratch using fresh ingredients to control salt and sugar levels.

Choose cooking oils that contain the least amount of trans-fat but high amounts of unsaturated fats, like olive oil, and coconut oil. Avoid cooking oils labeled 'hydrogenated' and 'partially hydrogenated'. Manufacturers of said products use the lowest quality of oils and treat these with industrial-strength solvents (e.g. hexane) to improve their color and smell. Unfortunately, regularly consuming these products can cause life-threatening diseases like cancer, coronary artery diseases, gallbladder disease, kidney failure, liver failure, and stroke. Research also shows that these products trigger chronic high cholesterol, diabetes mellitus, gout, hypertension, impaired fertility, joint diseases, and osteoarthritis.

Being Unprepared

The first thing you should do is to check your calendar. If you have a 'regular' week (e.g. no parties that require your attendance, or out-of-town trips, etc.), you can plan a week's worth of meals.

If the upcoming week is rather frantic, plan your meals accordingly but always have backup meals or snacks when you need to eat on the run. A good way to do so is to store fresh berries either in the fridge or freezer for making drinks or to consume as quick snacks. Cook soups or stews for several portions, and store these in freezer-safe containers, which can be reheated in the microwave as needed.

Keep extra containers of energy-boosting snacks in the pantry or in your bag (e.g. dehydrated mangoes, homemade energy bars, etc.) for quick pick-me-uppers.

Plan which dishes can be consumed for each meal, per day for the upcoming week, including beverages and snacks. Create, look up, and print corresponding recipes. This makes it easier to shop for food later.

Not making a detailed grocery list

Even with a sharp memory, it is still essential to create a grocery list before going to the stores. This helps limit food wastage and will prevent shopping over the budget. A detailed grocery list should include the name of the ingredient, the amount needed, and possible substitutes. This prevents the need to rework recipes if ingredients are not currently available.

Choosing dishes with hard to find ingredients

Although it is commendable to try out new ingredients and exotic dishes occasionally, it's always best to utilize local fresh produce for maximum taste and nutrient level. Whenever possible, take advantage of seasonal fruits and vegetables in your area. These are usually harvested at the peak of their flavor. And because there is a relatively larger supply than demand, prices will dip.

Before planning your meals and going grocery shopping, check the fridge and pantry for ingredients that can be incorporated in the week's meal plan. Items like canned beans, dried mushrooms, and homemade pickles have relatively long shelf lives and can be incorporated in numerous dishes. This helps lessen food wastage and saves a lot of money too.

Things to Put in Place before Getting Started with Meal Prepping

Get an Instant Pot and a Food Processor

An instant pot and a food processor will be your best companions. If you cannot afford a food processor, you can always rely on its cheaper version - the blender.

Get the right Kitchen Equipment

Measuring cups, measuring spoons, mixing bowls, vegetable peeler, sauce pans, stock pot, steamer, a good knife or two, mixing bowls; in small, medium and large sizes, mixing spoons, loaf pan, muffin tins, lasagna pan, cookie sheet, rolling pin, grater, cooling rack, whisk, colander, wax paper sifter, among others.

Keep a Rest/Sleep Schedule

If possible, aim for at least eight hours of good quality rest per night. When the body is asleep, consumed calories are converted into muscle energy faster.

Sleep speeds up the body's healing processes too, which improves the overall quality of hair, nails and skin. This is the time when the body processes out toxins from the system, which stabilizes bowel movement.

Aim to sleep and wake up at set hours each day or night. Establishing this routine will make the body acclimatize to lifestyle changes easier and faster.

When constantly waking up in the middle of the night, stay in bed. If there is a need to eat or drink something during this time, opt for a tall glass of water. If you must go to the bathrooms, then do so. Then go back to bed. Don't fiddle with your phone, or go online, as these activities will keep the brain awake for a longer time.

Some Meal Prep Success Tips

Here are some tips that will help you in your meal prep lifestyle

Learn to Store up in a Container

In order to pack a week's worth of meals, you are going to need a week's worth of containers. The easiest way to go about this to buy a set or two matching boxes which will make packing of prepared meals in the fridge easier for you. The containers must not match, you can also use mismatching containers. You will need smaller containers for storing salad dressings or dip.

Learn to Repeat Some Meals

In order to save time, repeat a few lunch components within a week. But space the repetition out throughout the week. For instance, your Tuesday's turkey wrap can also be packed for Friday's salad dip, etc.

Freeze up Things

Freezing is one of the best ways to store up food items without tampering with their nutritional values. For instance, freezing yogurt prevents them from sloshing about in the lunch box. The same applies to some other food items like apple sauce, corn peas, cooked edamame, etc.

Try to Figure Out Recipes that Can Last

It requires some trial and error to understanding what recipes are worthy of packing for a week's worth of launches. This study will also help you know how to fix those food stuffs that cannot last up to a week earlier in your week's food menu. (This is called strategic planning). For instance, sliced strawberries will be mushy by mid-week. So the best option is to fix them up in the Monday or Tuesday launch box.

Getting Started with Vegan and Vegetarian Meal Plans

Meal planning can be broken down into 5 simple steps.

Step 1: Talk with your family about foods they like. Think about how they can be a part of well-balanced meals that help you avoid high and low blood sugar levels.

Step 2: Shop at home. Before you head to the store or order your groceries for delivery, look at what you have at home. Do you need to use up produce before it spoils? Make a list of the foods you have on hand to help you choose recipes. Low on staples such as beans, oil, or pasta? Add them to your grocery list.

Step 3: Find recipes that match your family's tastes and your health goals. Start by looking at recipes you know your family loves. Are there ways to make them healthier? If you want to add new meals, save recipes from newspapers, magazines, or food blogs.

Step 4: Using what you learned in steps 1 to 3, fill out this meal planner pdf file at https://www.cdc.gov/diabetes/pdfs/prevent/Preventing-Diabetes-Meal-Planner.pdf to track what you plan to make and when. You can download, print and duplicate the meal planner file. The meal planner is also attached in this cookbook below. You can photocopy and duplicate the page.

Consider:

- Making meals during a time of day or day of the week when you are less rushed.
- Choosing one day to make meals in advance.
- Using a theme for each day of the week. Your family may enjoy the routine, and it can be fun! Meatless Mondays, Taco Tuesdays, or Whole-Grain Wednesdays are just a few ideas.

Step 5: Make your grocery list. Whether you use a pen and paper or an app, know what you need—and what you don't—before you shop.

Tips for the Kitchen

When you're ready to start cooking, here are some tips to make meal prep as easy and efficient as possible:

- Start with foods that will take the longest to cook, such as proteins like chicken, whole grains like brown rice, dried beans, and roasted vegetables.
- While foods are baking or simmering on the stovetop, wash and chop vegetables or prepare other foods that don't need to be cooked.
- Make extra portions of your recipe for leftovers. You can eat leftovers later in the week or use them to make a new meal. For example, try shredding leftover baked chicken and adding it to a stew, salad, or sandwich.
- Make quick snacks for the week, such as hard-boiled eggs, fresh cut fruit, or small salads. If you make a green salad that uses dressing, don't add the dressing until right before you eat it.
- Put servings of the prepared meal in individual containers. This helps with portions, and they're ready to grab if you pack your lunch.

Type 1 Diabetes Meal Plan Guide

The key to managing the diet with Type 1 Diabetes lies in balance and understanding how your body manages the glucose and insulin. It is possible to eat almost all foods that have been outlined in this cookbook, but the key is to understand how carbohydrates affect the diet.

It is carbohydrates that are converted into glucose most easily within the body. For glucose to be managed by insulin, an injection is administered. Being aware of how many carbohydrates you are consuming will make it easier for you to balance your insulin and control your blood glucose levels. The balance that is required is to eat generally the same amount of carbohydrates at the same times each day. Ideally, about a third of the plate should contain carbohydrates at the main meal of the day.

Rather than counting calories, a person with Type 1 Diabetes should seek the help of a healthcare professional who can teach them how to count carbohydrates. This will help with the management of diabetes in the long run, and teach the right approach to high carb meals.

The basic meal plan should follow these points:

- **Eat Three Meals Each Day:** These meals are breakfast, lunch and dinner. They should be eaten at approximately the same times each day. The key is to learn how to control your appetite, as well as your levels of blood glucose.

- **Consume Healthy Amounts of Fruits and Vegetables:** The standard quantity should be five portions in a day. These are important for the supply of vitamins and minerals that will balance the diet. In the morning, one can consume fresh or dried fruit; salads, vegetables and smoothies can also be used to meet the daily portions.
- **Avoid Cutting Out Carbohydrates:** Every meal should have some high fiber carbohydrates included. This is not only important for the maintenance of blood glucose levels, it is also required to prevent constipation. This will go a long way in maintaining the health of your digestive system.
- **Eat more Beans:** Beans are an excellent source of protein, and can easily be used as a substitute for meat. They are gentler on the digestive system, so more of them should be incorporated into the diet. They are also able to control the fats that are found in the blood.
- **Reduce your Fat Intake:** The body needs to have some fats for proper functioning, but these should be the right type of fats. Monounsaturated fats, healthy fats, are what the body needs. These can be found in olive oil or rapeseed oil, and in some fruits and nuts. Avocados and almonds are an excellent source of these fats. For the diabetic that needs to lose weight for better management of the disease, less fat should be consumed as this is the food group that contains the most calories.
- **Ensure that you Consume Oily Fish each Week:** A minimum of two portions of oily fish every week is recommended. These have omega 3 fatty acids, which help with the prevention of cardiovascular issues. The fish that should considered include sardines, pilchards and salmon.
- **Avoid Diabetic Foods and Drinks:** For the most part, these are a gimmick and may contain preservatives and other ingredients, which in the long run, may do more harm than good. They are also often overpriced and expensive to maintain for a daily diet. Either way, when consumed, they will still affect your blood glucose levels. Eating foods that are as natural as possible will be far more beneficial for your health and wellbeing.
- **Reduce your Salt Intake:** Too much salt is associated with many problems that can be caused by diabetes. This includes high blood pressure, as well as stroke and heart disease. Salt is primarily used as a flavoring for food. Rather than depending on salt, other flavorings can be considered, for example, herbs and spices.
- **Ensure that your Alcohol Consumption is in Moderation:** Avoid excessive consumption of alcohol. Alcohol is basically carbohydrates, which turns into glucose, and affects the blood glucose levels. At the most, one should consume a maximum of 2 units of alcohol per day for a woman and 3 units of alcohol per day as a man. However, if it is possible, alcohol should be avoided in its entirety to ensure that excellent health is maintained. If one must drink, it should never be on an empty stomach, as this can result in the occurrence of hypoglycemia and weight gain from empty calories.

Using these guidelines and eating the correct foods will lead to meals that are healthy and help with the management of the condition.

Type 2 Diabetes Meal Plan Guide

When one is diagnosed with diabetes and contemplating what food choices that they have left, they may feel that they are now limited. Considering that processed foods, including white flour, need to be eliminated from the diet, red meat and alcohol need to be drastically cut down, and sugary foods should be reduced as well, it may seem as though the variety that makes food delicious is no longer available to them.

This is not the case though, as managing Type 2 Diabetes through dieting requires one to eat a balanced diet. It really is quite simple. Foods need to be well thought out, and the nutritional aspect of every component in a meal given due consideration.

There should be a healthy variety of carbohydrates, proteins and fats. These make up the building blocks of what the body needs, so it can manage effectively. The right combination of these food groups will make all the difference. When there is imbalance, the possibility of experiencing diabetes symptoms becomes higher.

Understanding the roles that these foods play in the body will make a big difference to how they are consumed. Carbohydrates are broken down into glucose much faster than any of the other food groups. It is these foods that will impact the blood sugar levels. In the absence of carbohydrates, proteins and fats are able to impact blood sugar, but either way, they should be consumed in a controlled manner.

The typical plate for someone who has Type 2 Diabetes should be as follows. Half the plate should contain non-starchy vegetables (meaning no potatoes in this section). The rest of the plate should hold an assortment of whole grains or nuts and seeds, lean proteins, fruit, healthy fats and low fat dairy.

As much as is possible, sugar should be extremely limited. In addition to reducing your sugar intake, the intake of salt and fat should also be cut down. One should aim for developing their meal plan by incorporating foods that have high levels of fiber to replace those that have been excluded from the diet.

A good meal plan with a type 2 diabetic will result in excellent health. However, one should consider that a goal may be to reduce weight, particularly if that will alleviate the symptoms of the disease. If this is the case, what becomes important is not so much the food that is being eaten, but how it is being prepared. Food should be boiled or broiled as much as possible, or it should be grilled and roasted. As much as is possible, it should be consumed its natural or pure form, rather than with a considerable amount of additives.

The most important meal of the day is breakfast, as it is the first opportunity one has to balance the levels of glucose that are within the body.

What a Type 2 Diabetic Meal Plan is Not

This is not a meal plan that is about deprivation. As much as sugars are discouraged, they are not meant to be banned from the diet completely. What this meal plan calls for is moderate intake and proper planning to avoid foods that have hidden sugars, such as processed foods.

The diet is balanced, so it requires a dose of carbohydrates. One should not confuse the diet for diabetics with one for someone who is looking to shed some weight. They follow different principles. However, with the diabetic diet, one must focus on whole grains as the source of carbohydrates rather than processed grains.

It is not a meal plan that will lead to your exclusion from meal times with family. One can still eat normally, as long as moderation and nutritional consideration is taken seriously.

Gestational Diabetes Meal Plan Guide

If you have gestational diabetes, the main point to remember is that you require a diet that is nutritious. This requires a proper plan; if left untreated, gestational diabetes can affect the mother's health, as well as that of the baby. Babies can grow bigger than they are supposed to, leading to serious complications when it is time to give birth.

It is necessary to see a dietitian when one has gestational diabetes, as each case must be treated differently. There are certain things that need to be taken into consideration. These include the height and weight of the pregnant woman. The stage that she has reached in the pregnancy is important, as well as the level of physical activity that she has achieved. In addition to her needs, those of the growing baby must be met as well. On top of this, her personal food preferences are likely to be different in pregnancy.

Here are some pointers that are taken into consideration when preparing the meal plan.

- **First, the Number of Calories that are to be Consumed Each Day are Determined:** This will help in deciding what the portion sizes of the meals will be and how the balance of carbohydrates, proteins and fats can be presented. In addition, it is important that every meal also contains the appropriate amount of vitamins and minerals.
- **All Meals need to be Appropriately Balanced:** Ideally, a minimum of five meals should be consumed. These would be three main meals and two snacks throughout the day. Even the snacks need to be balanced in their nutritional make up. For some pregnant women with gestational diabetes, four snacks in addition to the three meals are recommended.
- A Woman with Gestational Diabetes cannot afford to Skip any of Her Meals or Cut Down on the Amount that needs to be consumed in Each Meal: Following a strict meal plan is the only way to ensure that the blood glucose levels have some stability. This will be possible of the meals are evenly spread out through the entire day.
- **The Meals may contain Lower Amounts of Carbohydrates than Normal:** The carbohydrates that are to be consumed will be complex to allow for a large amount of fiber. Pregnant women are already at risk of experiencing constipation, and this can become more severe if they do not get the right amount of fiber.
- **All proteins that are to be consumed will be lean**, and as there are less carbohydrates being consumed, more protein will help to sustain energy. This, in turn, will make it easier for the pregnant women to control her blood sugar.
- **The morning is the likely time during the day that blood glucose levels are likely to be their lowest.** Therefore, a hearty breakfast packed with nutrients is what the pregnant woman needs to consume. This breakfast should contain a limited amount of carbohydrates in the form of cereal and milk, but it should have a high amount of protein from eggs, cheese and peanut butter for example, and fruit juices should be avoided as much as possible.

Below are the meal plan samples for different diabetic lifestyles, for breakfast, lunch and dinner. Note that as a diabetic, you should always eat whenever you feel hungry. If you ever feel hungry in between the time for these standard meal, feel free to take any of the appetizers, sides or desserts in this cookbook. Eating fruits like apple, avocado, carrots, etc. is the best option for any time of the day. Always take note of the carbs and calories of what you consume, especially in between meals.

14 Days Meal Plan for Keto Dairy Free Vegan/Vegetarian Diet Lifestyle

Day 1

- **Breakfast:** Fried Up Avocados
- **Lunch:** Low Calorie Beets Dish
- **Dinner:** Cheesy Celery Croquettes with Chive Mayo

Day 2

- **Breakfast:** Permesan Cabbage Wedges
- **Lunch:** Cheesy Mushroom Slices
- **Dinner:** Broccoli with Garlic Sauce

Day 3

- **Breakfast:** Roasted Up Brussels
- **Lunch:** Fried Green Beans and Rosemary
- **Dinner:** Mini Portobello Mushroom Pizzas

Day 4

- **Breakfast:** Air Fried Beignets
- **Lunch:** Baked Cauliflower with Cheese
- **Dinner:** Greek Style Stuffed Eggplant

Day 5

- **Breakfast:** Chocolate Cake with Coconut Cream
- **Lunch:** Cheesy Eggplant Lasagna
- **Dinner:** Roasted Broccoli and Almond Salad

Day 6

- **Breakfast:** Vanilla Coconut Pie
- **Lunch:** Cauliflower Steak with Gremolata
- **Dinner:** Cheddar Cauliflower Pizza Crust

Day 7

- **Breakfast:** Zucchini Fries
- **Lunch:** Broccoli Cheese Fritters
- **Dinner:** Lemon Whole Roasted Cauliflower

Day 8

- **Breakfast:** Breaded Mushrooms
- **Lunch:** Roasted Spaghetti Squash
- **Dinner:** Vegetarian Parmesan Artichokes

Day 9

- **Breakfast:** Fried Parmesan Zucchini
- **Lunch:** Zucchini and Mushroom Kebab
- **Dinner:** Caprese Eggplant Stacks with Basil

Day 10

- **Breakfast:** Radish Chips
- **Lunch:** Eggplant with Tomato and Cheese
- **Dinner:** Broccoli Cheese Crust Pizza

Day 11

- **Breakfast:** Garlic Cheese Bread
- **Lunch:** Roasted Eggplant and Zucchini Bites
- **Dinner:** Hearty Garlic White Zucchini Rolls

Day 12

- **Breakfast:** Cinnamon Doughnuts
- **Lunch:** Cheesy Zucchini and Spinach
- **Dinner:** Mushroom and Zucchini Burgers

Day 13

- **Breakfast:** Creamed Spinach
- **Lunch:** Cheese Stuffed Zucchini
- **Dinner:** Green Cabbage Steaks

Day 14

- **Breakfast:** Squash and Cumin Chili
- **Lunch:** Ranch Cauliflower Patties
- **Dinner:** Brussels Sprouts with Toasted Pecan

7 Days Meal Plan for Vegan/Vegetarian Weight Watchers

Day 1

- **Breakfast:** Broccoli Quiche
- **Lunch:** Air Fried Fajitas
- **Dinner:** Black Bean Burger

Day 2

- **Breakfast:** Banana Bread
- **Lunch:** Saucy Carrots
- **Dinner:** Potato Cakes

Day 3

- **Breakfast:** Ranch Chickpeas
- **Lunch:** Veggie Bites
- **Dinner:** Lime Glazed Tofu

Day 4

- **Breakfast:** Battered Fried Tofu
- **Lunch:** Aubergine Fries
- **Dinner:** Quinoa Patties

Day 5

- **Breakfast:** Crunch Wrap
- **Lunch:** Apple Turnovers
- **Dinner:** Tofu Sandwich

Day 6

- **Breakfast:** Crostini with Hummus
- **Lunch:** Artichoke Hearts with Garlic Aioli
- **Dinner:** Crispy Avocado Tacos

Day 7

- **Breakfast:** Popcorn Tofu Nuggets
- **Lunch:** Mushroom Capsicum Kabobs
- **Dinner:** Buffalo Cauliflower Steaks

14 Days Meal Plan for Vegan/Vegetarian Diabetics

Day 1

- **Breakfast:** Shoestring Butternut Squash Fries
- **Lunch:** Air Fried Cheesy Onions
- **Dinner:** Pepper Jack Cauliflower Bites

Day 2

- **Breakfast:** Roasted Peppers with Balsamic Vinegar and Basil
- **Lunch:** Sauteed Mushrooms
- **Dinner:** Mint-Butter Stuffed Mushrooms

Day 3

- **Breakfast:** Sweet Potato Curly Fries
- **Lunch:** Easy Cheesy Broccoli
- **Dinner:** Gorgonzola Stuffed Mushrooms with Horseradish Mayo

Day 4

- **Breakfast:** Roasted Yellow Squash and Onions
- **Lunch:** Stuffed Mushrooms
- **Dinner:** Orange Tofu

Day 5

- **Breakfast:** Fried Cauliflower with Parmigiano-Reggiano Lemon Dressing
- **Lunch:** Mediterranean Halloumi and Garlic Omelet
- **Dinner:** Golden Turmeric Cauliflower Steaks

Day 6

- **Breakfast:** Roman Artichokes
- **Lunch:** Roma Tomato Bites with Halloumi Cheese
- **Dinner:** Portobello Mushrooms with Hummus Sauce

Day 7

- **Breakfast:** Eggplants with Garlic and Parsley
- **Lunch:** Indian-Style Garnet Sweet Potatoes
- **Dinner:** Toasted Coconut French Toast

Day 8

- **Breakfast:** Potato Appetizer with Garlic-Mayo Sauce
- **Lunch:** Easy Sautéed Green Beans
- **Dinner:** Pecan French Toast

Day 9

- **Breakfast:** Roasted Cauliflower with Garlic and Capers
- **Lunch:** Easy Cheesy Cauliflower and Broccoli
- **Dinner:** Oatmeal with Raspberries

Day 10

- **Breakfast:** Tandoori Cauliflower
- **Lunch:** Greek-Style Mushrooms
- **Dinner:** Corn Muffins

Day 11

- **Breakfast:** Tomato Candy
- **Lunch:** Veggie Fried Rice
- **Dinner:** Avocado Fries

Day 12

- **Breakfast:** Roasted Garlic and Thyme Tomatoes
- **Lunch:** Crisp Banana Chips
- **Dinner:** Corn Tortilla Chips

Day 13

- **Breakfast:** Vegan Breakfast Ranchero
- **Lunch:** Buffalo Tofu
- **Dinner:** Cauliflower Chickpea Tacos

Day 14

- **Breakfast:** Vegetable Couscous

- **Lunch:** Sweet Potato-Cinnamon Toast
- **Dinner:** Mediterranean-Style Frittata with Manchego

Jenny Crawford

Meal Planner for Diabetics

Feel free to photocopy and duplicate this meal planner page.

Meal Planner

Week of: _____

	Monday	Tuesday	Wednesday	Thursday	Friday	Saturday	Sunday
Breakfast							
Lunch							
Dinner							

Meal Planner – Source: cdc.gov

Altrnatively, you can download the PDF file at **https://www.cdc.gov/diabetes/pdfs/prevent/Preventing-Diabetes-Meal-Planner.pdf**.

CONCLUSION

Once more, thanks for purchasing this *Essential Vegan & Vegetarian Air Fryer Cookbook UK*. The low carb vegan and vegetarian air fryer recipes in this cookbook will help you eat healthily, no matter the category of vegan and vegetarian low carb meal you eat; weight watcher, diabetic, ketogenic; dairy-free, etc.

If you found this cookbook helpful, don't hesitate to drop your testimonies on the Amazon page of this cookbook. Enjoy!

Printed in Great Britain
by Amazon